MEDITERRANEAN DIET SLOW COOKER COOKBOOK

MEDITERRANEAN DIET
SLOW COOKER
COOKBOOK

100 Healthy Recipes

SHANNON EPSTEIN

PHOTOGRAPHY BY THOMAS J. STORY

ROCKRIDGE
PRESS

For general information on our other products and services or to obtain technical support, please contact our Customer Care Department within the United States at (866) 744-2665, or outside the United States at (510) 253-0500.

Rockridge Press publishes its books in a variety of electronic and print formats. Some content that appears in print may not be available in electronic books, and vice versa.

Interior and Cover Designer: John Clifford
Art Producer: Sara Feinstein
Editor: Laura Bryn Sisson
Production Editor: Mia Moran

Photography © 2019 Thomas J. Story. Food styling by Alexa Hyman.
Author photo © Joshua Monesson, Monesson Photography

Cover: Cioppino, p. 78

ISBN: Print 978-1-64152-940-2 | eBook 978-1-64152-941-9

R0

Thank you to everyone
who has supported me
through this journey.

Contents

Introduction

Almost a decade ago, I dedicated myself to a healthier lifestyle and I have not looked back since. I have tried every diet under the sun—from Paleo to low-carb to keto. They all work well for me and, to be honest, most days I eat on the spectrum of all of them. Having said that, there is a reason the Mediterranean diet is consistently listed as one of the best and easiest diets to follow—because it is how we all should eat. The Mediterranean diet's emphasis on vegetables, fruits, fish, lean meats, good fats such as olive oil, and healthy legumes just flat-out makes sense.

I have appreciated Mediterranean food my entire life, but I fell in love with it after my visit to Israel in 2012 and then Greece the next year. I could not believe how fresh the dishes were while offering so much flavor. For a week straight, I ate a combination of fresh fish, vegetables, lean meats, and wholesome grains. For the first time, I came home from vacation without gaining a ton of weight. Don't get me wrong, I gained a little—but only because the food was so good that I could not help but overindulge at times. You know the saying, "When in Rome . . . "? It's true.

When I got home from my travels, I was determined to recreate some of the food I ate on my trip—in the slow cooker, of course. It is no secret that I love my slow cooker; this is my fourth slow-cooker cookbook and I have an entire blog dedicated to slow cooking. I quickly discovered that slow cookers are great for making Mediterranean food! Ingredients such as lentils and lamb are perfect for the set-it-and-forget-it, low-and-slow method of slow cooking. Fish and other seafood . . . not so much. Even though some of those recipes have a shorter cook time than what you may be used to with slow cooking, the result is still an easy, delicious, healthy meal.

Mediterranean countries are those that surround the Mediterranean Sea, and they include Spain, France, Italy, Greece, Turkey, Lebanon, Morocco, Tunisia, Malta, and Cyprus—among others. These diverse countries each have their own cuisine and distinctive take on the Mediterranean diet. Although this book does not include recipes inspired by all of them, I have tried to provide a broad variety of dishes to please different palates.

I hope this cookbook shows you a different way to slow-cook and opens your eyes to the wonders of the Mediterranean diet. I will talk about what the Mediterranean diet is, why it is beneficial, and how to properly use your slow cooker to create its recipes, even if you are making your own recipe and not using one from this cookbook. To be honest, creating some of these recipes took me out of my comfort zone at times, but, in the end, I could not be happier with the results. Writing this cookbook made me remember why I love Mediterranean food in the first place. If you are not a Mediterranean food lover (yet), I hope you soon will be.

SLOW COOKING THE MEDITERRANEAN WAY

I am a firm believer that almost anything can be made in the slow cooker. Foods for the Mediterranean diet are no different. In this chapter, I discuss which foods can be eaten on the Mediterranean diet and which are best for slow cooking, as well as what to avoid and which foods must be prepared with special cooking instructions. And even those recipes (seafood, for example) are simple ones that you can make with minimal fuss.

WHAT IS THE MEDITERRANEAN DIET?

In 2019, the *U.S. News and World Report* released their Best Diets rankings for the year. The panel—comprising experts on heart disease, diabetes, nutrition, food psychology, and obesity—reviewed research about diets from all over the world. To no one's surprise, the Mediterranean diet came in at number one.

Considered a lifestyle more than a diet, the Mediterranean way of eating is almost universally considered the way we all should eat daily. As I previously mentioned, many countries make up the Mediterranean region, each with their own cuisine, which further proves my point that this is not really a specific diet to follow but more of a way to live. It emphasizes eating foods such as fish, other seafood, fruits, vegetables, nuts, legumes, whole grains, beans, and olive oil—all seasoned naturally with herbs and spices. Also allowed are poultry, red meat, eggs, cheese, and yogurt—and the occasional glass of red wine. Yes, you read that correctly. The Mediterranean diet allows wine! I will discuss more about that later.

The main principle of the Mediterranean diet is to eat whole foods, and processed foods with added sugars, refined grains, and refined oils are out. But I think we can all agree that we should not be eating foods with these ingredients on a regular basis anyway.

Low-carb diets restrict carbs. Paleo diets restrict legumes. Weight Watchers® restricts calories. With the Mediterranean diet, food is not restricted and calories are not counted. Its principles are to eat well and stay physically active on an almost daily basis. Because food groups are not restricted, the Mediterranean diet is easier to follow than other diets. Again, an occasional glass of wine is not only allowed but also encouraged!

Following a Mediterranean way of eating is also cost-effective. For example, you do not necessarily have to buy an expensive piece of salmon; tuna is an acceptable and very affordable option. Dried lentils can be purchased in the bulk-item section at your local grocery store for a couple of dollars per pound—sometimes even less.

In addition to weight loss, eating the Mediterranean way has many other health benefits. It is common knowledge that people who live around the

Mediterranean Sea tend to live longer and have fewer cardiovascular diseases than people in other countries. The Mediterranean diet is a big factor in this because of its daily encouragement to lead a balanced, healthy lifestyle.

EAT A LOT OF . . .

What can you eat? On this first tier of the Mediterranean diet, you can have as much as your heart desires of the following foods:

- **VEGETABLES:** The sky is the limit when it comes to eating vegetables. Vegetables are not only full of nutritional value, but they are also versatile and can be eaten at every meal, including breakfast. Grill, sauté, steam, or eat them raw. A good way to get your daily servings is to add vegetables to your grains and legumes or make a fresh salad topped with your favorite protein.

- **WHOLE GRAINS:** Don't be afraid of carbs! Whole grains such as brown rice, quinoa, farro, and bulgur are great sources of fiber and are also known to reduce blood cholesterol levels and lower the risk of heart disease.

- **NUTS AND SEEDS:** Nuts and seeds are highly nutritious and have been shown to reduce the risk of coronary artery disease. You can eat them by themselves or incorporate them into recipes. Common nuts and seeds in the Mediterranean diet include almonds, cashews, chestnuts, pine nuts, pistachios, and walnuts, as well as sesame and sunflower seeds.

- **FRUIT:** Most fruits contain sugar, but some types have more of it than others. Eating fruit is a good way to satisfy your fix for something sweet without relying on processed foods or foods with added refined sugars. Try to eat locally grown fruits whenever possible. Because locally grown produce doesn't have far to travel, local farms can allow it to fully ripen, which adds to its nutritional value. Without that long travel time and distance, greenhouse gas emissions are reduced, which is better for the environment. And, most importantly, eating local produce supports local farmers. Avocados, tomatoes, grapes, figs, dates, prunes, olives, and more are all good fruit choices for this diet.

- **LEGUMES:** Legumes such as chickpeas (also known as garbanzo beans), lentils, peas, and navy beans are great sources of protein, fiber, and vitamin B, which is why they are commonly used in vegetarian and vegan diets.

- **OLIVE OIL:** Olive oil is the go-to fat in the Mediterranean diet, whether it is used as a dressing or a cooking oil. Olive oil contains high amounts of antioxidants that have anti-inflammatory properties. Choosing an olive oil can be tricky because many variables go into producing a good grade, and unfortunately, no universal system exists to properly compare these grades. Good-quality olive oil does taste better and has more health benefits, but it can also be more expensive. Before investing in an olive oil, I suggest you do a bit of research to find a type that fits not just your dietary needs but your budget and palate as well.

- **FISH AND SEAFOOD:** Fish and shellfish are excellent sources of protein and are packed with omega-3 fatty acids. Terrific choices include salmon, shrimp, tuna, cod, and even anchovies. Avoid seafood that tends to be high in mercury, such as swordfish.

EAT SOME OF . . .

This second tier of the Mediterranean diet includes foods that can be eaten a couple of times a week. While poultry and dairy are allowed on the Mediterranean diet, they should be eaten in moderation. A good way to incorporate these items is to eat a small portion along with vegetables, whole grains, and legumes.

- **CHEESE:** Although cheese is allowed, choose unprocessed cheeses such as feta, Parmesan, and ricotta.

- **EGGS:** Eat whole eggs, not just the whites. Although egg whites are lower in cholesterol and calories, the yolks offer many valuable nutrients.

- **POULTRY:** Meats such as chicken, turkey, quail, and Cornish game hens are lean proteins that can be eaten once or twice a week. Both white meat (think breasts) and dark meat (think legs and thighs) are allowed.

- **YOGURT:** Stick to Greek yogurt, which is strained to remove the excess liquid known as whey; this reduces the amount of lactose sugar.

EAT LESS OF . . .

The great thing about the Mediterranean diet is that it is pretty inclusive. Even though you must limit your intake of heavily processed foods, there is still a lot you can eat.

- **RED MEAT:** Red meats such as beef, lamb, and pork are allowed. But they can sometimes be high in saturated fats, so it's best to eat red meat in moderation. Lamb is a popular meat in the Mediterranean region.

- **DESSERT:** Avoid store-bought desserts because of their processed ingredients and added sugars. Homemade desserts are okay to indulge in occasionally. Choose desserts that incorporate fresh fruits and vegetables, use olive oil or yogurt instead of lots of butter, and include whole-wheat flour instead of white flour.

- **NATURAL SUGARS:** Although you should try to stay away from things like candy, store-bought baked goods, and soda, natural sugars are okay in moderation. Get your sweet-tooth fix by eating fruit or using honey in your baked goods.

- **WINE:** A diet you can drink wine on! But don't overdo it. It is recommended that you consume a quantity less than or equal to one or two drinks per day for men and one drink per day for women. The recommended serving size for one drink of wine is five ounces.

EAT NONE OF . . .

In general, you should stay away from all processed foods or foods with added sugar. Read labels; if you cannot pronounce an ingredient, avoid the product. When you shop for groceries, stick to the outer perimeter of the store, where the departments for fresh produce, meats, and fish are located.

- **REFINED GRAINS:** White flour, white bread, crackers, pasta made with refined wheat, pastries, and cereals contain virtually no beneficial vitamins, minerals, or fiber.

- **ADDED SUGARS:** Avoid soda, candy, and store-bought cakes and desserts. Beware: Processed foods labeled "no-fat" or "low-fat" are usually high in added sugars.

- **PROCESSED MEAT:** Processed meats such as hot dogs, cold cuts, and deli meats (even nitrate-free ones) are often full of additives and fillers.

- **REFINED OILS:** Not all oil is the same. Refined oils are usually made using a chemical solvent or are sometimes chemically altered. Avoid oils such as canola, corn, cottonseed, peanut, rapeseed, safflower, soybean, sunflower, and vegetable oil.

THE MEDITERRANEAN DIET FOOD PYRAMID

The Mediterranean Diet Pyramid is a nutrition guide that was developed in the early 1990s by the Oldways Preservation Trust, the Harvard School of Public Health, and the World Health Organization. It visually summarizes the Mediterranean diet pattern of what to eat and includes examples of the diet's foods and serving frequencies.

- The top of the pyramid represents the foods you should eat daily: fruits, vegetables, whole grains, legumes, nuts, seeds, herbs, spices, and good fats such as olive oil. These plant-based foods and healthy fats should be worked into every meal, if possible.

- As you move down the pyramid, limit your intake of the items listed. The second tier is fish and seafood, which should be eaten at least twice a week.

- Following that is dairy, which is eaten frequently but in moderate portions, along with poultry and eggs.

- At the bottom of the pyramid are red meats, sweets, and processed foods, which should be extremely limited or avoided.

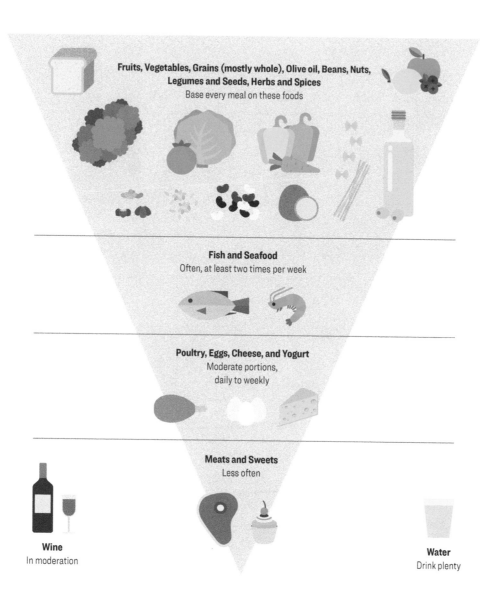

Fruits, Vegetables, Grains (mostly whole), Olive oil, Beans, Nuts, Legumes and Seeds, Herbs and Spices
Base every meal on these foods

Fish and Seafood
Often, at least two times per week

Poultry, Eggs, Cheese, and Yogurt
Moderate portions,
daily to weekly

Meats and Sweets
Less often

Wine
In moderation

Water
Drink plenty

HEALTH BENEFITS OF THE MEDITERRANEAN DIET

Eating the Mediterranean diet and living the Mediterranean lifestyle (which includes exercise) have many benefits. Recent studies cited in the *U.S. News and World Report* show that the Mediterranean diet can result in weight loss and helps prevent heart attacks, strokes, type 2 diabetes, and premature death. The Mediterranean diet is not only good for your physical health but also your mental health.

- High-fiber diets help prevent swings in your blood-sugar levels; this in turn helps you lower your risk of diabetes and maintain a healthy weight.

- Limiting your intake of red meat, processed foods, and refined breads can help prevent heart disease and strokes.

- Spending time outdoors and exercising in general are simple, effective ways to reduce stress and anxiety as well as help fight against disease.

- The Mediterranean diet can help you improve your overall "good" cholesterol levels, maintain appropriate blood sugar levels, and support blood vessel health.

THE MEDITERRANEAN LIFESTYLE

The Mediterranean diet is about more than just eating wholesome foods—it is also about changing your lifestyle.

- **EAT SLOWLY.** A central principle of Mediterranean living is to enjoy life—not rush through it. Typical Mediterranean meals can last for hours. Rather than quickly and automatically shoveling food into your mouth, eat mindfully and enjoy the companionship of the meal as well.

- **GET SOCIAL.** Mediterranean people are some of the most social I have ever met. Have a meal with a group of friends. Healthy social interactions are known to lower blood pressure and help you live longer. A positive time with friends (or even strangers) can do wonders for your psyche.

- **MOVE.** Exercise is encouraged, but that does not mean you have to spend hours at the gym. Most Mediterranean countries have weather that allows inhabitants to get outside frequently, which is why walking is a big part of the Mediterranean lifestyle. Walking is a good way to start increasing the amount of exercise you get and it also encourages you to go outside and enjoy nature. Adults are encouraged to get about three hours of moderate-intensity activity each week.

- **SHOP OUTDOORS.** Visiting a local farmers' market is a good way to pick up locally sourced foods and get outside.

Slow Cooker 101

New to slow cooking? Don't be intimidated. Slow cookers are one of the easiest appliances to use. Here are some tips to keep you successful:

- Buy the right-size appliance. If you are a household of two or fewer, I suggest a 3½-quart slow cooker. Larger families will need to invest in a 6-quart cooker.

- Invest in a programmable slow cooker if you plan to let it cook while you are gone. Yes, manual slow cookers are cheaper but they are also that: manual. The good thing about programmable slow cookers is that they will either shut off or turn themselves to the Warm setting once the cook time is complete. This makes it less likely to overcook or burn your food.

- Use your appliance year-round. Although some people slow-cook only during the fall and winter months, slow cookers emit little to no heat, so they are great for summer months when it is too hot to use the oven.

TAKE IT SLOW

There are many reasons to use your slow cooker for Mediterranean cooking, even if they are not obvious. Slow cooking is wholesome and cost-effective. Slow-cooker recipes use practical ingredients and produce healthy meals with minimal effort. Making your own meals also gives you complete control over what you are eating—in this case, using Mediterranean diet–approved foods.

Processed foods are not needed to make a good slow-cooker meal. In fact, it is the opposite. Fresh ingredients, like vegetables and healthy proteins, are cooked to perfection in the slow cooker. What I love most about slow cookers is the minimal prep involved. You can make delicious lentils with chicken and vegetables by throwing everything together, giving the ingredients a stir, and letting the meal cook on its own. If you want to make your meal in advance, a lot of slow-cooker recipes make good freezer meals. This means you can prep your recipe when you have some extra time, put it in the freezer, and, when you are ready, thaw it in the refrigerator the night before you are ready to serve it, and cook it in the slow cooker the next day.

Plus, the low-and-slow cooking method really brings out the flavors in food. Grains and legumes cook with minimal effort. Your meats become fall-apart tender. Slow cooking with the Mediterranean diet is a foolproof way to assist you in living a healthier lifestyle—and eating some great food too.

THE BEST SLOW FOODS

Certain foods are better suited for the slow cooker than others—mainly those that require long cooking times:

- **DRIED BEANS:** Dried beans are less expensive and healthier than processed canned beans, which can be high in sodium. They also hold their form and texture better than canned beans in slow cooking and are less likely to get mushy if overcooked. And, the best part about cooking dried beans in the slow cooker? *You do not have to soak them first.* Give them a good rinse and add them right to the slow cooker. (Red kidney beans are an exception—they always need soaking.)

- **GRAINS AND LEGUMES:** Long-cooking grains (such as rice and barley) and legumes (such as lentils) are perfect for the slow cooker and require minimal prep and no presoaking.

- **HERBS:** Herbs are a great way to add flavor to a dish. Most of these recipes call for dried herbs because they are cheaper and last longer. However, you can use fresh herbs in their place at any time.

- **INEXPENSIVE CUTS OF MEAT:** Due to the low-and-slow cooking method, even the toughest cuts of meat come out of the slow cooker melt-in-your-mouth tender. Therefore, you can use cheaper cuts like chicken thighs and tough cuts of lamb, beef, and pork with exceptional results, such as beef chuck roast, beef brisket, lamb shank, or pork shoulder or butt.

- **ROOT VEGETABLES:** Sturdy vegetables such as parsnips, carrots, and beets are great for slow cooking because they require a longer cooking time to become tender.

- **WAXY POTATOES:** Waxy-textured potatoes are best for slow cooking because they hold their shape better after a long cooking time. If you use nonwaxy potatoes, cut them into larger chunks than usual; this helps prevent them from turning to mush during cooking.

Embrace Canned Tomatoes!

Canned tomatoes are commonly used in slow cooking. Canned tomatoes are a cost-effective way to add tomatoes (and their health benefits) into your recipes, especially when fresh tomatoes are not in season. When you buy canned tomatoes, read the ingredients list and look for those that are all-natural and have no added salt. You can always add salt to a dish to taste, but you do not need it from canned tomatoes. If the ingredients listed are just tomatoes, tomato juice, calcium chloride, and citric acid, they are a good choice.

SLOW LIKE A PRO

Here are some tips to have you slow-cooking like a pro in no time:

- **DO NOT OVERCROWD THE SLOW COOKER.** Slow cookers do their thing on their own but they also need the chance to work properly. Overstuffing one results in unevenly cooked food and it is an easy way to ruin a dish.

- **DO NOT REMOVE THE LID.** Not even for a peek! A lot of people don't know this, but removing the lid releases a lot of heat. If you do it, you add as many as 30 more minutes of cooking time to the dish because the food and the cooker need to return to their former temperature.

- **CUT YOUR FOOD INTO EQUAL PIECES.** Cutting your food into uniform sizes helps it cook evenly.

- **TRIM OFF THE FAT FROM THE MEAT.** Of course, a little fat is good and adds flavor. But too much fat will make the slow cooker full of grease (and this is not really encouraged on the diet).

- **USE THE CORRECT-SIZE SLOW COOKER.** You do not want to use a slow cooker that is too big for the food you are cooking. Try to fill your slow cooker at least 75 percent full; otherwise you risk burning the food.

Use the Right Slow Cooker

With the exception of the dessert recipes, all of the other recipes in this book are intended to be cooked in a 5- or 6-quart cooker. If you are using a smaller-size slow cooker, simply halve the recipe. For the cakes in the dessert chapter, it is your choice whether to use a 5- or 6-quart slow cooker, or a 3½-quart one. A smaller slow cooker will produce a taller cake. The other desserts should be made in a 3½-quart slow cooker.

ABOUT THE RECIPES

I tried as much as possible to provide a wide range of recipes that represents the many countries of the Mediterranean region, and to use ingredients that are readily available in our local grocery stores. There, you will find all the common ingredients that make the Mediterranean diet popular: chickpeas, lentils, eggs, chicken, and more. Olive oil is also in almost every recipe—even in a couple of cakes that feature it as a main ingredient. Each recipe comes with insights and tips to help you adjust and modify it to suit your taste buds or dietary needs. Nutritional calculations are provided for your convenience, but I encourage you not to focus on counting calories on this diet.

Most of the recipes adhere to the true set-it-and-forget-it style of slow cooking we all love. That's the point of a slow cooker, right? You turn it on before work and come home to an amazing meal. The cook times in these recipes are generally 6 to 8 hours, but there are some exceptions. With poultry, dark meat is better for slow cooking, so it is used frequently. White meat cooks faster than dark meat, so if you prefer it, you should reduce the cook time by an hour or so to ensure that it does not dry out.

The main exceptions to the long cook times are seafood and desserts. Seafood is such a staple in the Mediterranean diet that I have devoted an entire chapter to it, but it also cooks quickly. If you were to cook seafood on low heat for 6 to 8 hours, it would turn either tough and rubbery or mushy. You will find that for seafood recipes, the cook times are a few hours shorter than in other recipes.

Regarding desserts, cake batters can be cooked in the slow cooker but, like seafood, they do not take that long. I don't want you to eat burnt dessert, so you will find that these cooking times are shorter.

White Bean Soup,
page 22

SOUPS AND STEWS

MEDITERRANEAN VEGETABLE SOUP

SERVES 6 // PREP TIME: 20 MINUTES // COOK TIME: 6 TO 8 HOURS ON LOW

Grab your favorite Mediterranean vegetables for this easy, light, and healthy soup recipe. Don't like mushrooms? Omit them! Simply add different vegetables, like asparagus.

1 (28-ounce) can no-salt-added diced tomatoes

2 cups low-sodium vegetable broth

1 green bell pepper, seeded and chopped

1 red or yellow bell pepper, seeded and chopped

4 ounces mushrooms, sliced

2 zucchini, chopped

1 small red onion, chopped

3 garlic cloves, minced

1 tablespoon extra-virgin olive oil

2 teaspoons dried oregano

1 teaspoon paprika

1 teaspoon sea salt

½ teaspoon freshly ground black pepper

Juice of 1 lemon

1. In a slow cooker, combine the tomatoes, vegetable broth, green and red bell peppers, mushrooms, zucchini, onion, garlic, olive oil, oregano, paprika, salt, and black pepper. Stir to mix well.

2. Cover the cooker and cook for 6 to 8 hours on Low heat.

3. Stir in the lemon juice before serving.

INGREDIENT TIP: Experiment with the ratio of diced tomatoes to broth. For a less tomato-based soup, use 1 (15-ounce) can no-salt-added diced tomatoes and 4 cups vegetable broth.

Per Serving: Calories: 91; Total fat: 3g; Sodium: 502mg; Carbohydrates: 16g; Fiber: 5g; Sugar: 9g; Protein: 3g

HERBED SALMON AND KALE SOUP

SERVES 6 // PREP TIME: 10 MINUTES // COOK TIME: 3 TO 5 HOURS ON LOW

Salmon paired with kale and herbs produces a light and healthy soup that can be enjoyed year-round. Kale is packed with minerals and vitamins, but its leaves can be on the tough side. Adding the kale at the beginning of the cook time will make it more tender and easier to digest.

2 pounds fresh salmon fillets, cut into 2-inch pieces

1 cup chopped kale

3 cups low-sodium vegetable broth or low-sodium chicken broth

4 cups water

1 small onion, diced

½ cup diced carrot

2 garlic cloves, minced

1 teaspoon dried parsley

1 teaspoon dried oregano

1 teaspoon dried thyme

1 teaspoon sea salt

¼ teaspoon freshly ground black pepper

1. In a slow cooker, combine the salmon, kale, vegetable broth, water, onion, carrot, garlic, parsley, oregano, thyme, salt, and pepper. Stir to mix well.

2. Cover the cooker and cook for 3 to 5 hours on Low heat.

INGREDIENT TIP: If you do not like salmon, substitute a different fish such as trout or arctic char.

Per Serving: Calories: 212; Total fat: 6g; Sodium: 471mg; Carbohydrates: 6g; Fiber: 2g; Sugar: 2g; Protein: 32g

LENTIL SOUP

SERVES 6 // PREP TIME: 10 MINUTES // COOK TIME: 6 TO 8 HOURS ON LOW

Lentils are a staple in Mediterranean cooking. I could not write a Mediterranean cookbook without an easy lentil soup. You can use either green or red lentils for this hearty soup, which can be served as a starter or a main dish.

1 cup dried red or green lentils, rinsed well under cold water and picked over to remove debris

4 cups low-sodium vegetable broth

4 cups water

1 small onion, diced

2 carrots, diced

2 celery stalks, diced

1 cup fresh spinach, chopped

1 teaspoon dried oregano

1 teaspoon ground cumin

1 teaspoon paprika

1 teaspoon sea salt, plus more as needed

¼ teaspoon freshly ground black pepper, plus more as needed

Juice of 1 lemon

1. In a slow cooker, combine the lentils, vegetable broth, water, onion, carrots, celery, spinach, oregano, cumin, paprika, salt, and pepper. Stir to mix well.
2. Cover the cooker and cook for 6 to 8 hours on Low heat.
3. Stir in the lemon juice. Taste and add more seasoning, if needed, before serving.

PREPARATION TIP: If you like a smoother texture, purée the soup in a blender (or use an immersion blender) until smooth.

Per Serving: Calories: 130; Total fat: 1g; Sodium: 514mg; Carbohydrates: 23g; Fiber: 11g; Sugar: 5g; Protein: 9g

LEMON CHICKEN SOUP WITH ORZO

SERVES 6 // PREP TIME: 10 MINUTES // COOK TIME: 6 TO 8 HOURS ON LOW, PLUS 15 TO 30 MINUTES ON LOW FOR THE ORZO

Orzo resembles grains of rice, but it is actually small rice-shaped pasta. It is commonly used in Italian recipes, particularly soups. This simple citrus-flavored soup can be served as a main course.

1 pound boneless, skinless chicken thighs or 1 pound bone-in, skinless chicken breast

4 cups low-sodium chicken broth

2 cups water

2 celery stalks, thinly sliced

1 small onion, diced

1 carrot, diced

1 garlic clove, minced

Grated zest of 1 lemon

Juice of 1 lemon

1 bay leaf

1 teaspoon sea salt

1 teaspoon dried oregano

½ teaspoon freshly ground black pepper

¾ cup dried orzo pasta

1 lemon, thinly sliced

1. In a slow cooker, combine the chicken, chicken broth, water, celery, onion, carrot, garlic, lemon zest, lemon juice, bay leaf, salt, oregano, and pepper. Stir to mix well.
2. Cover the cooker and cook for 6 to 8 hours on Low heat.
3. Remove the chicken from the slow cooker and shred it. (If you are using bone-in chicken, remove and discard the bones while shredding. The meat should be so tender that the bones just slide out.)
4. Return the chicken to the slow cooker and add the orzo and lemon slices.
5. Replace the cover on the cooker and cook for 15 to 30 minutes on Low heat, or until the orzo is tender.
6. Remove and discard the bay leaf before serving.

INGREDIENT TIP: If you cannot find orzo, use your preferred dried pasta. You can use riced cauliflower instead if you prefer a lighter version of this soup that is lower in calories, low-carb, and Paleo.

Per Serving: Calories: 195; Total fat: 5g; Sodium: 561mg; Carbohydrates: 22g; Fiber: 3g; Sugar: 2g; Protein: 15g

CREAM OF ZUCCHINI SOUP

If you do not like zucchini, this soup is not for you. Zucchini is the main ingredient, but the herbs are what really bring out the flavor. Traditionally this soup is served warm, but it can also be served cold if you prefer.

4 zucchini, cut into ½-inch chunks

4 cups low-sodium vegetable broth

1 small onion, diced

1 garlic clove, minced

1 teaspoon sea salt

¼ teaspoon freshly ground black pepper

¼ teaspoon dried thyme

¼ teaspoon dried rosemary

¼ teaspoon dried basil

½ cup plain Greek yogurt

1. In a slow cooker, combine the zucchini, vegetable broth, onion, garlic, salt, pepper, thyme, rosemary, and basil. Stir to mix well.
2. Cover the cooker and cook for 6 to 8 hours on Low heat.
3. Stir in the yogurt.
4. Using an immersion blender, purée the soup until smooth. Or, transfer the soup to a standard blender, working in batches as needed, and blend until smooth.

INGREDIENT TIP: Use your favorite creamy thickener instead of yogurt—such as heavy (whipping) cream, half-and-half, or even coconut milk.

Per Serving: Calories: 55; Total fat: 2g; Sodium: 507mg; Carbohydrates: 9g; Fiber: 2g; Sugar: 5g; Protein: 3g

GREEK SALAD SOUP

SERVES 6 // PREP TIME: 15 MINUTES // COOK TIME: 6 TO 8 HOURS ON LOW

There is a reason why the classic Greek salad is so popular—it is not only simple to make but it is also full of flavor. This recipe takes all the ingredients of a Greek salad but turns them into a tasty soup. This light, healthy soup can be served year-round.

4 tomatoes, cut into wedges

2 cucumbers, cut into 1-inch-thick rounds

2 green bell peppers, seeded and diced

1 small red onion, diced

1 cup whole Kalamata olives, pitted

4 cups low-sodium chicken broth

2 cups water

1 tablespoon extra-virgin olive oil

2 teaspoons red wine vinegar

1½ teaspoons dried oregano

1 teaspoon sea salt

½ teaspoon freshly ground black pepper

4 ounces feta cheese, crumbled

1. In a slow cooker, combine the tomatoes, cucumbers, bell peppers, onion, olives, chicken broth, water, olive oil, vinegar, oregano, salt, and black pepper. Stir to mix well.

2. Cover the cooker and cook for 6 to 8 hours on Low heat.

3. Top each bowl with feta cheese before serving.

INGREDIENT TIP: Make this a heartier soup by stirring in 1 cup of your favorite cooked pasta once the cook time is complete. If you have leftover cooked chicken, put it in along with the vegetables in step 1.

Per Serving: Calories: 180; Total fat: 12g; Sodium: 976mg; Carbohydrates: 13g; Fiber: 3g; Sugar: 4g; Protein: 6g

WHITE BEAN SOUP

SERVES 6 // PREP TIME: 10 MINUTES // COOK TIME: 6 TO 8 HOURS ON LOW

Also known as *fasolada* or *fasoulada*, this Greek soup consists of white beans and vegetables. It is a simple, common soup that is easy to make—but do not be surprised if you also find it on the menu at an upscale Greek restaurant.

1 pound dried white
beans, rinsed

4 cups water

1 (15-ounce) can no-salt-added
diced tomatoes

2 celery stalks, diced

1 cup diced carrot

1 small onion, diced

2 garlic cloves, minced

1 teaspoon dried parsley

1 teaspoon dried thyme

1 teaspoon sea salt

½ teaspoon freshly ground
black pepper

2 bay leaves

1. In a slow cooker, combine the beans, water, tomatoes, celery, carrot, onion, garlic, parsley, thyme, salt, pepper, and bay leaves. Stir to mix well.

2. Cover the cooker and cook for 6 to 8 hours on Low heat.

3. Remove and discard the bay leaves before serving.

PREPARATION TIP: Make this soup spicy by adding ½ to 1 teaspoon red pepper flakes with the other spices. Try garnishing with fresh thyme and black pepper.

Per Serving: Calories: 282; Total fat: 1g; Sodium: 462mg; Carbohydrates: 53g; Fiber: 21g; Sugar: 6g; Protein: 19g

MINCED BEEF OR LAMB SOUP

SERVES 6 // PREP TIME: 20 MINUTES // COOK TIME: 6 TO 8 HOURS ON LOW

This hearty soup is simple and yet full of flavor. It will also fill your entire kitchen with enticing aromas while it cooks. You can use ground beef or lamb in this recipe, whichever you prefer.

1 pound raw ground beef or lamb

12 ounces new red potatoes, halved, or 1 (15-ounce) can reduced-sodium chickpeas, drained and rinsed

4 cups low-sodium beef broth

2 cups water

2 carrots, diced

2 celery stalks, diced

2 zucchini, cut into 1-inch pieces

1 large tomato, chopped

1 small onion, diced

2 garlic cloves, minced

¼ cup no-salt-added tomato paste

1 teaspoon sea salt

1 teaspoon dried oregano

1 teaspoon dried basil

½ teaspoon freshly ground black pepper

½ teaspoon dried thyme

2 bay leaves

1. In a large skillet over medium-high heat, cook the ground meat for 3 to 5 minutes, stirring and breaking it up with a spoon until it has browned and is no longer pink. Drain any grease and put the meat in a slow cooker.

2. Add the potatoes, beef broth, water, carrots, celery, zucchini, tomato, onion, garlic, tomato paste, salt, oregano, basil, pepper, thyme, and bay leaves to the ground meat. Stir to mix well.

3. Cover the cooker and cook for 6 to 8 hours on Low heat.

4. Remove and discard the bay leaves before serving.

INGREDIENT TIP: Use poultry in this recipe in place of the red meat. Ground chicken or ground turkey can be substituted without making any changes to the cook time.

Per Serving: Calories: 200; Total fat: 6g; Sodium: 790mg; Carbohydrates: 20g; Fiber: 4g; Sugar: 5g; Protein: 20g

MOROCCAN FISH STEW

This recipe is tailored for *you*. I purposefully kept the title generic—"fish stew"—because you can use any preferred fish in this recipe. Cod, sea bream, mullet, sea bass, and mackerel are all Mediterranean fish that work well. And you do not necessarily have to use a Mediterranean fish—tilapia, halibut, or salmon are also delicious in this stew.

1 pound fresh fish fillets of your choice, cut into 2-inch pieces

3 cups low-sodium vegetable broth or low-sodium chicken broth

1 (15-ounce) can no-salt-added diced tomatoes

1 bell pepper, any color, seeded and diced

1 small onion, diced

1 garlic clove, minced

1 teaspoon ground coriander

1 teaspoon sea salt

1 teaspoon paprika

½ teaspoon ground turmeric

½ teaspoon freshly ground black pepper

¼ cup fresh cilantro

1. In a slow cooker, combine the fish, vegetable broth, tomatoes, bell pepper, onion, garlic, coriander, salt, paprika, turmeric, and black pepper. Stir to mix well.
2. Cover the cooker and cook for 3 to 5 hours on Low heat.
3. Garnish with the fresh cilantro for serving.

SERVING TIP: Serve this stew over cooked rice (either white or brown) or even riced cauliflower for a light meal.

Per Serving: Calories: 115; Total fat: 1g; Sodium: 547mg; Carbohydrates: 8g; Fiber: 3g; Sugar: 4g; Protein: 18g

CHICKPEA STEW

Chickpeas are another ingredient that is commonly used in Mediterranean cooking. Also known as garbanzo beans, chickpeas are a part of the legume family. They are a nutrient-dense food high in protein and fiber. Serve this vegan stew over cooked brown rice or couscous, or as is.

2 cups dried chickpeas, rinsed

4 cups low-sodium vegetable broth or low-sodium chicken broth

1 tablespoon extra-virgin olive oil

1 small onion, diced

1 green bell pepper, seeded and chopped

2 garlic cloves, minced

1 tablespoon drained capers

1 teaspoon ground cumin

1 teaspoon ground turmeric

½ teaspoon ground coriander

½ teaspoon sea salt

¼ teaspoon freshly ground black pepper

1. In a slow cooker, combine the chickpeas, vegetable broth, olive oil, onion, bell pepper, garlic, capers, cumin, turmeric, coriander, salt, and black pepper. Stir to mix well.

2. Cover the cooker and cook for 6 to 8 hours on Low heat.

INGREDIENT TIP: Canned chickpeas are also okay to use in this recipe. Buy a reduced-sodium version and drain and rinse them well before adding to the slow cooker.

Per Serving: Calories: 286; Total fat: 6g; Sodium: 347mg; Carbohydrates: 45g; Fiber: 13g; Sugar: 9g; Protein: 14g

Za'atar Chickpeas and Chicken,
page 33

BEANS AND GRAINS

FALAFEL

Falafel is a popular vegetarian Mediterranean staple made from ground chickpeas, onions, and seasonings, and sometimes other ingredients like eggs and bread crumbs. Traditionally the ingredients are ground together and then lightly fried. A more basic version of falafel appeared in my first cookbook, *The Easy & Healthy Slow Cooker Cookbook*. This version is slightly different because it uses fresh herbs and different seasonings. Enjoy this vegan falafel year-round.

Nonstick cooking spray

2 cups canned reduced-sodium chickpeas, rinsed and drained

4 garlic cloves, peeled

¼ cup chickpea flour or all-purpose flour

¼ cup diced onion

¼ cup chopped fresh parsley

¼ cup chopped fresh cilantro

1 teaspoon sea salt

1 teaspoon ground cumin

½ teaspoon ground coriander

½ teaspoon freshly ground black pepper

⅛ teaspoon cayenne pepper

1. Generously coat a slow cooker insert with cooking spray.
2. In a blender or food processor, combine the chickpeas, garlic, flour, onion, parsley, cilantro, salt, cumin, coriander, black pepper, and cayenne pepper. Process until smooth. Form the mixture into 6 to 8 (2-inch) round patties and place them in a single layer in the prepared slow cooker.
3. Cover the cooker and cook for 6 to 8 hours on Low heat.

SERVING TIP: Eat this falafel as is, or serve it in a warm pita bread with lettuce, tomato, and tahini sauce.

Per Serving: Calories: 174; Total fat: 3g; Sodium: 594mg; Carbohydrates: 30g; Fiber: 8g; Sugar: 5g; Protein: 9g

MEDITERRANEAN LENTIL CASSEROLE

SERVES 6 // PREP TIME: 15 MINUTES // COOK TIME: 8 TO 10 HOURS ON LOW

Lentils come in many forms, including brown, green, red, yellow, and more. In this vegan recipe, you can use whatever kind of lentil you prefer or have on hand. Because of their tiny size, you do not need to soak them before adding them to the slow cooker.

1 pound lentils, rinsed well under cold water and picked over to remove debris

4 cups low-sodium vegetable broth

3 carrots, diced

3 cups chopped kale

1 small onion, diced

2 garlic cloves, minced

1 teaspoon sea salt

1 teaspoon dried basil

1 teaspoon dried oregano

½ teaspoon dried parsley

1 lemon, thinly sliced

1. In a slow cooker, combine the lentils, vegetable broth, carrots, kale, onion, garlic, salt, basil, oregano, and parsley. Stir to mix well.
2. Cover the cooker and cook for 8 to 10 hours on Low heat, or until the lentils are tender.
3. Garnish with lemon slices for serving.

SERVING TIP: Garnish this lentil casserole with your favorite toppings, such as chopped fresh mint, cilantro, or even a simple yogurt sauce.

Per Serving: Calories: 302; Total fat: 2g; Sodium: 527mg; Carbohydrates: 54g; Fiber: 26g; Sugar: 7g; Protein: 22g

BLACK-EYED PEAS WITH HAM

Although they are called black-eyed *peas*, they are really beans! This is a traditionally Southern recipe that has been given a Mediterranean overhaul here. *Ras al-hanout* is a common Moroccan spice blend that consists of many ingredients, including ginger, cinnamon, cloves, and cumin. It is a bitter yet sweet spice that is very aromatic and can be used on almost anything from meats to vegetables to rice. This recipe lists the ingredients to make your own homemade blend, but if you have store-bought ras al-hanout in your cupboard, use 3 tablespoons of that in place of the individual spices called for here (except the garlic). If you cannot find a ham hock, use 2 cups of chopped ham instead.

FOR THE RAS AL-HANOUT

1 teaspoon ground cumin

1 teaspoon ground ginger

1 teaspoon ground turmeric

1 teaspoon paprika

1 teaspoon garlic powder

1 teaspoon red pepper flakes

½ teaspoon ground cinnamon

½ teaspoon ground coriander

½ teaspoon ground nutmeg

½ teaspoon ground cloves

½ teaspoon sea salt

½ teaspoon freshly ground black pepper

FOR THE STEW

1 pound dried black-eyed peas, rinsed well under cold water and picked over to remove debris

1 large ham hock

5 cups low-sodium chicken broth

1 small onion, diced

1 bell pepper, any color, seeded and diced

2 garlic cloves, minced

TO MAKE THE RAS AL-HANOUT

In a small bowl, combine the cumin, ginger, turmeric, paprika, garlic powder, red pepper flakes, cinnamon, coriander, nutmeg, cloves, salt, and black pepper. Mix thoroughly.

TO MAKE THE STEW

1. In a slow cooker, combine the black-eyed peas, ham hock, chicken broth, onion, bell pepper, garlic, and the ras al-hanout. Stir to mix well.

2. Cover the cooker and cook for 6 to 8 hours on Low heat.

PREPARATION TIP: If you prefer a smoother texture in this dish: When cooking is complete, remove 1 cup of the peas, mash them thoroughly, and stir them back into the mixture.

Per Serving: Calories: 456; Total fat: 18g; Sodium: 295mg; Carbohydrates: 58g; Fiber: 22g; Sugar: 3g; Protein: 37g

PORK AND WHITE BEAN STEW

White beans are a good source of fiber and vitamin B. In this recipe, use your favorite white bean—whether cannellini, great northern, or navy. This simple recipe uses affordable ingredients that produce a hearty yet healthy stew.

2 pounds boneless pork shoulder or butt, cut into 1-inch cubes

1 (15-ounce) can reduced-sodium white beans, drained and rinsed

2 cups low-sodium vegetable broth or low-sodium chicken broth

1 (15-ounce) can no-salt-added diced tomatoes

1 small onion, diced

2 garlic cloves, minced

1½ teaspoons dried rosemary

1 teaspoon sea salt

½ teaspoon freshly ground black pepper

4 ounces fresh spinach, chopped

1. In a slow cooker, combine the pork, beans, vegetable broth, tomatoes, onion, garlic, rosemary, salt, and pepper. Stir to mix well.

2. Cover the cooker and cook for 6 to 8 hours on Low heat.

3. Stir in the spinach, replace the cover on the cooker, and cook for 15 to 30 minutes on Low heat, or until the spinach wilts.

INGREDIENT TIP: You can substitute dried beans (about ¾ cup) for the canned beans. If you do, you do not need to soak them first; rinse them and add them directly to the slow cooker.

Per Serving: Calories: 370; Total fat: 19g; Sodium: 575mg; Carbohydrates: 17g; Fiber: 6g; Sugar: 4g; Protein: 32g

ZA'ATAR CHICKPEAS AND CHICKEN

Za'atar is a spice blend commonly used in Middle Eastern cooking, popular in countries such as Egypt, Morocco, Jordan, Lebanon, and Turkey. It is a mixture of thyme, oregano, marjoram, sesame seeds, salt, and sumac (an edible red berry with a tart, lemony flavor). Za'atar can be used on pretty much anything—meat, vegetables, and even mixed into dips.

2 pounds bone-in chicken thighs or legs

1 (15-ounce) can reduced-sodium chickpeas, drained and rinsed

½ cup low-sodium chicken broth

Juice of 1 lemon

1 tablespoon extra-virgin olive oil

2 teaspoons white vinegar

2 tablespoons za'atar

1 garlic clove, minced

½ teaspoon sea salt

¼ teaspoon freshly ground black pepper

1. In a slow cooker, combine the chicken and chickpeas. Stir to mix well.
2. In a small bowl, whisk together the chicken broth, lemon juice, olive oil, vinegar, za'atar, garlic, salt, and pepper until combined. Pour the mixture over the chicken and chickpeas.
3. Cover the cooker and cook for 4 to 6 hours on Low heat.

INGREDIENT TIP: You can use chicken breast for this recipe instead of thighs or legs. Use the same amount and reduce the cook time by 1 hour or so. Otherwise, you risk overcooking the chicken (and no one likes dried-out chicken!).

Per Serving: Calories: 647; Total fat: 41g; Sodium: 590mg; Carbohydrates: 23g; Fiber: 7g; Sugar: 4g; Protein: 46g

LENTIL BOWL

SERVES 6 // PREP TIME: 10 MINUTES // COOK TIME: 6 TO 8 HOURS ON LOW

This is another easy vegan lentil one-pot meal. But if you are not worried about keeping this recipe vegan or vegetarian, you can stir in up to 12 ounces of cooked meat, like ground lamb, at the beginning of the cook time. Serve this lentil bowl with your favorite cooked rice.

1 cup dried lentils, any color, rinsed well under cold water and picked over to remove debris

3 cups low-sodium vegetable broth

1 (15-ounce) can no-salt-added diced tomatoes

1 small onion, chopped

3 celery stalks, chopped

3 carrots, chopped

3 garlic cloves, minced

2 tablespoons Italian seasoning

1 teaspoon sea salt

½ teaspoon freshly ground black pepper

2 bay leaves

1 tablespoon freshly squeezed lemon juice

1. In a slow cooker, combine the lentils, vegetable broth, tomatoes, onion, celery, carrots, garlic, Italian seasoning, salt, pepper, and bay leaves. Stir to mix well.

2. Cover the cooker and cook for 6 to 8 hours on Low heat.

3. Stir in the lemon juice before serving.

INGREDIENT TIP: Instead of the Italian seasoning, you can use finely chopped fresh herbs such as parsley, thyme, oregano, or basil. You will need 6 tablespoons total.

Per Serving: Calories: 152; Total fat: 1g; Sodium: 529mg; Carbohydrates: 29g; Fiber: 13g; Sugar: 7g; Protein: 10g

FAVA BEANS WITH GROUND MEAT

SERVES 6 // PREP TIME: 15 MINUTES // COOK TIME: 6 TO 8 HOURS ON LOW

Fava beans are green legumes that are popular in many Mediterranean and Middle Eastern recipes. You can use canned or dried fava beans in this recipe. If you use canned favas, drain and rinse them first. If you use dried, get ones that are preskinned or have the shells removed. For the ground meat, use whatever you prefer—lamb, beef, chicken, turkey, or even pork.

8 ounces raw ground meat

1 pound dried fava beans, rinsed well under cold water and picked over to remove debris, or 1 (15-ounce) can fava beans, drained and rinsed

10 cups water or 5 cups water and 5 cups low-sodium vegetable broth

1 small onion, diced

1 bell pepper, any color, seeded and diced

1 teaspoon sea salt

1 teaspoon garlic powder

1 teaspoon dried parsley

1 teaspoon dried oregano

1 teaspoon paprika

1 teaspoon cayenne pepper

½ teaspoon freshly ground black pepper

½ teaspoon dried thyme

1. In a large skillet over medium-high heat, cook the ground meat for 3 to 5 minutes, stirring and breaking it up with a spoon, until it has browned and is no longer pink. Drain any grease and put the meat in a slow cooker.
2. Add the fava beans, water, onion, bell pepper, salt, garlic powder, parsley, oregano, paprika, cayenne pepper, black pepper, and thyme to the meat. Stir to mix well.
3. Cover the cooker and cook for 6 to 8 hours on Low heat, or until the beans are tender.

VARIATION TIP: Make this dish vegan by using 1 cup dried lentils of any color instead of the ground meat.

Per Serving: Calories: 308; Total fat: 4g; Sodium: 417mg; Carbohydrates: 43g; Fiber: 19g; Sugar: 5g; Protein: 26g

BARLEY AND VEGETABLE CASSEROLE

Barley is a whole grain that is high in fiber and important vitamins and minerals. It is a versatile grain that can be used in many recipes. Mixing barley with your favorite Mediterranean vegetables and seasonings makes an easy, filling casserole that can be served for family dinner or a work potluck.

1 cup raw barley (not the quick-cooking type)

3 cups low-sodium vegetable broth

3 garlic cloves, minced

2 bell peppers, any color, seeded and chopped

1 small onion, chopped

2 ounces mushrooms, sliced

1 teaspoon extra-virgin olive oil

2 tablespoons Italian seasoning

1 teaspoon sea salt

¼ teaspoon freshly ground black pepper

1. In a slow cooker, combine the barley, vegetable broth, garlic, bell peppers, onion, mushrooms, olive oil, Italian seasoning, salt, and black pepper. Stir to mix well.

2. Cover the cooker and cook for 6 to 8 hours on Low heat.

INGREDIENT TIP: If you do not have fresh vegetables on hand, use frozen ones and follow the recipe as written.

Per Serving: Calories: 147; Total fat: 2g; Sodium: 464mg; Carbohydrates: 30g; Fiber: 8g; Sugar: 3g; Protein: 5g

BULGUR-STUFFED PORTOBELLO MUSHROOMS

SERVES 4 // PREP TIME: 15 MINUTES // COOK TIME: 6 TO 8 HOURS ON LOW

Bulgur is a type of parched, cracked wheat that is popular in Mediterranean and Middle Eastern cooking. Its nutty flavor can be paired with pretty much anything from vegetables to meat. Because this recipe uses 4 portobello mushrooms, you will need a large slow cooker that holds 5 to 6 quarts for the mushrooms to fit properly. Halve the recipe if you have only a smaller 3½-quart cooker.

1½ cups cooked bulgur

2 zucchini, diced

¼ cup diced onion

2 garlic cloves, minced

1 teaspoon sea salt

1 teaspoon ground cumin

½ teaspoon freshly ground black pepper

1 (28-ounce) can no-salt-added crushed tomatoes

4 portobello mushrooms, stemmed, gills removed, wiped clean

1. In a medium bowl, stir together the bulgur, zucchini, onion, garlic, salt, cumin, and pepper.
2. Put the tomatoes in a slow cooker.
3. Evenly stuff each portobello mushroom cap with the bulgur mixture. Place the mushrooms on top of the tomatoes in a single layer.
4. Cover the cooker and cook for 6 to 8 hours on Low heat.

INGREDIENT TIP: Make this into a casserole using *raw* bulgur and chopped portobello mushrooms. Mix everything together and let it cook as directed.

Per Serving: Calories: 144; Total fat: 1g; Sodium: 688mg; Carbohydrates: 32g; Fiber: 9g; Sugar: 11g; Protein: 7g

HERBED POLENTA

Polenta is a popular Italian ingredient made from ground yellow corn. Although it is usually served as a side dish or accompaniment, this hearty polenta recipe is a terrific vegetarian main dish. Omit the cheese and opt for vegetable stock, and the recipe is vegan.

1 cup stone-ground polenta

4 cups low-sodium vegetable stock or low-sodium chicken stock

1 tablespoon extra-virgin olive oil

1 small onion, minced

2 garlic cloves, minced

1 teaspoon sea salt

1 teaspoon dried parsley

1 teaspoon dried oregano

1 teaspoon dried thyme

½ teaspoon freshly ground black pepper

½ cup grated Parmesan cheese

1. In a slow cooker, combine the polenta, vegetable stock, olive oil, onion, garlic, salt, parsley, oregano, thyme, and pepper. Stir to mix well.

2. Cover the cooker and cook for 3 to 5 hours on Low heat.

3. Stir in the Parmesan cheese for serving.

INGREDIENT TIP: Polenta is very similar to grits except grits are usually made from ground white corn. If you cannot find polenta, use grits instead and follow the recipe as written.

Per Serving: Calories: 244; Total fat: 7g; Sodium: 956mg; Carbohydrates: 33g; Fiber: 4g; Sugar: 3g; Protein: 9g

Rigatoni with Lamb Meatballs,
page 57

RICE AND PASTA

HERBED FISH CASSEROLE WITH RICE

SERVES 4 // PREP TIME: 10 MINUTES // COOK TIME: 2 TO 4 HOURS ON LOW

Simple herbs cook with brown rice and cod in this easy slow-cooker recipe. Brown rice works best with slow cooking, so I do not recommend using white rice here. Fresh cod holds its texture better than frozen; if fresh is not available, frozen cod can be used but it needs to be thawed first before putting in the slow cooker. The finished casserole is creamy, more like a risotto in texture than a crispy rice dish.

Nonstick cooking spray

1 cup raw long-grain brown rice, rinsed

2½ cups low-sodium chicken broth

1 tablespoon freshly squeezed lemon juice

2 garlic cloves, minced

1 teaspoon sea salt

1 teaspoon dried oregano

1 teaspoon dried parsley

1 teaspoon dried basil

1 teaspoon dried thyme

½ teaspoon onion powder

½ teaspoon freshly ground black pepper

1 pound fresh cod fillets

1. Generously coat a slow cooker insert with cooking spray. Put the rice, chicken broth, lemon juice, garlic, salt, oregano, parsley, basil, thyme, onion powder, and pepper in a slow cooker, and stir to mix well.

2. Place the cod fillets on top of the rice mixture.

3. Cover the cooker and cook for 2 to 4 hours on Low heat.

INGREDIENT TIP: Garnish this rice with a crumbly cheese such as feta. You can also substitute another sturdy fish, such as sea bass, if you prefer.

Per Serving: Calories: 296; Total fat: 3g; Sodium: 716mg; Carbohydrates: 38g; Fiber: 3g; Sugar: <1g; Protein: 31g

CHICKEN CASSEROLE WITH RICE

SERVES 4 // PREP TIME: 15 MINUTES // COOK TIME: 3 TO 5 HOURS ON LOW

Mediterranean flavors cook with the chicken in this rice casserole, which can be served at any time of the year, any day of the week. This one-pot dish is full of your favorite Mediterranean ingredients like tomatoes, olives, and capers.

Nonstick cooking spray

1 cup raw long-grain brown rice, rinsed

2½ cups low-sodium chicken broth

1 small onion, diced

4 garlic cloves, minced

1 teaspoon extra-virgin olive oil

2 Roma tomatoes, chopped

4 ounces whole Kalamata olives, pitted

2 tablespoons drained capers

1 teaspoon sea salt

1 teaspoon ground cumin

½ teaspoon freshly ground black pepper

1½ pounds bone-in, skin-on chicken thighs

1 lemon, thinly sliced

¼ cup chopped fresh basil

¼ cup crumbled feta cheese

1. Generously coat a slow-cooker insert with cooking spray. Put the rice, chicken broth, onion, garlic, olive oil, tomatoes, olives, capers, salt, cumin, and pepper in a slow cooker. Stir to mix well.
2. Nestle the chicken thighs into the rice mixture and top with lemon slices.
3. Cover the cooker and cook for 3 to 5 hours on Low heat.
4. Garnish with the fresh basil and feta for serving.

INGREDIENT TIP: To reduce the fat content of this dish, use boneless, skinless chicken thighs instead of bone-in, if you prefer. Once the chicken is done cooking, remove it from the cooker, shred it, and stir it back into the rice.

PREPARATION TIP: If you prefer a crispier chicken skin, once the cook time is complete, remove the bone-in chicken pieces from the slow cooker, place them on a baking sheet, and put them under the broiler for 5 minutes or so.

Per Serving: Calories: 684; Total fat: 39g; Sodium: 1,502mg; Carbohydrates: 49g; Fiber: 5g; Sugar: 4g; Protein: 37g

CHICKEN ARTICHOKE RICE BAKE

SERVES 4 // PREP TIME: 10 MINUTES // COOK TIME: 3 TO 5 HOURS ON LOW

Chicken, artichokes, rice, and spinach cook together in this easy, flavorful casserole bake. After cooking, the chicken will be so tender that it will shred easily. Stir the shredded chicken back into the rice for a one-pot meal.

Nonstick cooking spray

1 cup raw long-grain brown rice, rinsed

2½ cups low-sodium chicken broth

1 (14-ounce) can artichoke hearts, drained and rinsed

½ small onion, diced

2 garlic cloves, minced

10 ounces fresh spinach, chopped

1 teaspoon dried thyme

½ teaspoon sea salt

½ teaspoon freshly ground black pepper

1 pound boneless, skinless chicken breast

1. Generously coat a slow-cooker insert with cooking spray. Put the rice, chicken broth, artichoke hearts, onion, garlic, spinach, thyme, salt, and pepper in a slow cooker. Gently stir to mix well.
2. Place the chicken on top of the rice mixture.
3. Cover the cooker and cook for 3 to 5 hours on Low heat.
4. Remove the chicken from the cooker, shred it, and stir it back into the rice in the cooker.

VARIATION TIP: Make this a cheesy dish by stirring in 1 cup shredded mozzarella cheese at the beginning of the cook time.

Per Serving: Calories: 323; Total fat: 4g; Sodium: 741mg; Carbohydrates: 44g; Fiber: 6g; Sugar: 2g; Protein: 32g

RICE WITH BLACKENED FISH

SERVES 4 // PREP TIME: 10 MINUTES // COOK TIME: 2 TO 4 HOURS ON LOW

An easy homemade blackening seasoning is the star of this recipe. Make this a spicy dish by adding 1 teaspoon (or more) of red pepper flakes to the blackening seasoning.

1 teaspoon ground cumin

1 teaspoon ground coriander

1 teaspoon garlic powder

1 teaspoon paprika

½ teaspoon sea salt

½ teaspoon freshly ground black pepper

½ teaspoon onion powder

1 pound fresh salmon fillets

1 cup raw long-grain brown rice, rinsed

2½ cups low-sodium chicken broth

¼ cup diced tomato

1. In a small bowl, stir together the cumin, coriander, garlic powder, paprika, salt, pepper, and onion powder. Generously season the salmon fillets with the blackening seasoning.
2. In a slow cooker, combine the rice, chicken broth, and tomato. Stir to mix well.
3. Place the seasoned salmon on top of the rice mixture.
4. Cover the cooker and cook for 2 to 4 hours on Low heat.

INGREDIENT TIP: Use frozen salmon if you like! No adjustments to the recipe are needed—just add the blackening seasoning to the outside of the frozen salmon and place the frozen fillets on top of the rice mixture as instructed.

Per Serving: Calories: 318; Total fat: 6g; Sodium: 337mg; Carbohydrates: 38g; Fiber: 3g; Sugar: <1g; Protein: 29g

RICE WITH PORK CHOPS

Pork chops and Mediterranean-flavored rice cook together in this easy meal with minimal prep. Mediterranean herbs such as oregano and basil add a different taste to this basic pork-chop-and-rice recipe. Use bone-in or boneless pork chops, whichever you prefer.

1 cup raw long-grain brown rice, rinsed

2½ cups low-sodium chicken broth

1 cup sliced tomato

8 ounces fresh spinach, chopped

1 small onion, chopped

2 garlic cloves, minced

2 teaspoons dried oregano

2 teaspoons dried basil

1 teaspoon sea salt

½ teaspoon freshly ground black pepper

4 thick-cut pork chops

¼ cup grated Parmesan cheese

1. In a slow cooker, combine the rice, chicken broth, tomato, spinach, onion, garlic, oregano, basil, salt, and pepper. Stir to mix well.
2. Place the pork chops on top of the rice mixture.
3. Cover the cooker and cook for 3 to 5 hours on Low heat.
4. Top with the Parmesan cheese for serving.

INGREDIENT TIP: If you do not eat pork, use chicken thighs (boneless or bone-in) instead. Chicken breasts are not recommended because they will dry out during the long cook time.

Per Serving: Calories: 375; Total fat: 10g; Sodium: 1,042mg; Carbohydrates: 43g; Fiber: 6g; Sugar: 1g; Protein: 31g

MEDITERRANEAN "FRIED" RICE

SERVES 4 // PREP TIME: 15 MINUTES // COOK TIME: 3 TO 5 HOURS ON LOW, PLUS 15 TO 30 MINUTES ON LOW FOR THE EGGS

While this dish is technically not fried rice, it borrows the same concept with Mediterranean flavors. To make the rice more crispy after it is done slow cooking, transfer it to a wok and stir-fry it with 1 tablespoon extra-virgin olive oil over medium heat for 5 to 10 minutes, stirring frequently.

Nonstick cooking spray

1 cup raw long-grain brown rice, rinsed

2½ cups low-sodium chicken broth

2 tablespoons extra-virgin olive oil

2 tablespoons balsamic vinegar

2 zucchini, diced

4 ounces mushrooms, diced

1 small onion, diced

2 garlic cloves, minced

1 carrot, diced

1 bell pepper, any color, seeded and diced

¼ cup peas (raw, frozen, or canned)

1 teaspoon sea salt

1 pound boneless, skinless chicken breast, cut into ½-inch pieces

2 large eggs

1. Generously coat a slow-cooker insert with cooking spray. Put the rice, chicken broth, olive oil, vinegar, zucchini, mushrooms, onion, garlic, carrot, bell pepper, peas, and salt in a slow cooker. Stir to mix well.

2. Nestle the chicken into the rice mixture.

3. Cover the cooker and cook for 3 to 5 hours on Low heat.

4. In a small bowl, whisk the eggs. Pour the eggs over the chicken and rice. Replace the cover on the cooker and cook for 15 to 30 minutes on Low heat, or until the eggs are scrambled and cooked through.

5. Fluff the rice with a fork before serving.

PREPARATION TIP: Save some time by stirring in previously cooked scrambled eggs once the chicken and rice have finished cooking. Or, if you choose to add the step of making the rice crispier, add the raw eggs to the wok and cook them while stir-frying.

Per Serving: Calories: 431; Total fat: 14g; Sodium: 876mg; Carbohydrates: 48g; Fiber: 5g; Sugar: 5g; Protein: 35g

EASY CHICKEN AND RICE

SERVES 4 // PREP TIME: 10 MINUTES // COOK TIME: 3 TO 5 HOURS ON LOW

This family-friendly chicken and rice recipe is basic but a crowd-pleaser. You can jazz this up by adding 1 cup of your favorite chopped vegetables and also different seasonings. Don't have any oregano on hand? Use dried thyme or rosemary.

1 cup raw long-grain brown rice, rinsed

2½ cups low-sodium chicken broth

1 small onion, diced

2 garlic cloves, minced

1 teaspoon dried oregano

1 teaspoon dried parsley

1 teaspoon sea salt

½ teaspoon freshly ground black pepper

1½ pounds bone-in, skin-on chicken thighs

1. In a slow cooker, combine the rice, chicken broth, onion, garlic, oregano, parsley, salt, and pepper. Stir to mix well.
2. Nestle the chicken on top of the rice mixture.
3. Cover the cooker and cook for 3 to 5 hours on Low heat.

PREPARATION TIP: If you prefer a crispier chicken skin, once the cook time is complete, remove the chicken from the slow cooker, place it on a baking sheet, and put it under the broiler for 5 minutes or so.

Per Serving: Calories: 546; Total fat: 27g; Sodium: 755mg; Carbohydrates: 38g; Fiber: 3g; Sugar: 1g; Protein: 35g

LEMON RICE PILAF

SERVES 4 // PREP TIME: 10 MINUTES // COOK TIME: 3 TO 5 HOURS ON LOW

This lemony rice pilaf is a great option for vegans, vegetarians, or Meatless Mondays. You can play around with its citrus flavors by using 1 lemon and 1 orange, or 1 lemon and 1 lime. Serve this as an entrée or as a side dish with your favorite Mediterranean chicken, fish, or beef recipe.

1 cup raw long-grain brown rice, rinsed

2½ cups low-sodium vegetable broth

Juice of 2 lemons

1 teaspoon grated lemon zest

1 small onion, diced

2 garlic cloves, minced

1 teaspoon sea salt

1 teaspoon dried dill

2 tablespoons fresh parsley

1. In a slow cooker, combine the rice, vegetable broth, lemon juice, lemon zest, onion, garlic, salt, and dill. Stir to mix well.
2. Cover the cooker and cook for 3 to 5 hours on Low heat.
3. Garnish with the fresh parsley for serving.

VARIATION TIP: If you don't want to keep this recipe vegetarian, make it a complete one-pot recipe by stirring in 8 ounces cooked, chopped chicken after the cook time is complete.

Per Serving: Calories: 186; Total fat: 2g; Sodium: 628mg; Carbohydrates: 40g; Fiber: 3g; Sugar: 1g; Protein: 6g

PASTA CASSEROLE WITH SPINACH AND FETA

SERVES 4 // PREP TIME: 10 MINUTES // COOK TIME: 3 TO 5 HOURS ON LOW

The key to cooking pasta in the slow cooker is to have enough sauce to cover it. This ensures that it cooks until tender. Use 8 ounces of your preferred pasta in this recipe—whether it is rigatoni, spaghetti, or even macaroni.

Nonstick cooking spray

8 ounces dried pasta

2 (28-ounce) cans no-salt-added crushed tomatoes

2 cups fresh spinach, chopped

4 ounces mushrooms, sliced

3 garlic cloves, minced

1½ teaspoons dried parsley

1 teaspoon dried basil

1 teaspoon sea salt

½ teaspoon freshly ground black pepper

½ cup crumbled feta cheese, divided

1. Generously coat a slow-cooker insert with cooking spray. Put the pasta, tomatoes, spinach, mushrooms, garlic, parsley, basil, salt, pepper, and ¼ cup of feta cheese in a slow cooker. Stir to mix well.
2. Cover the cooker and cook for 3 to 5 hours on Low heat or until the pasta is tender.
3. Garnish with the remaining ¼ cup feta cheese for serving.

VARIATION TIP: Stir in 8 ounces of raw chopped chicken or raw or cooked ground beef in step 1.

Per Serving: Calories: 363; Total fat: 5g; Sodium: 984mg; Carbohydrates: 67g; Fiber: 9g; Sugar: 17g; Protein: 15g

GNOCCHI WITH SAUSAGE

SERVES 6 // PREP TIME: 10 MINUTES // COOK TIME: 4 TO 6 HOURS ON LOW,
PLUS 15 TO 30 MINUTES ON LOW FOR THE GNOCCHI AND KALE

I consider this dish Italian comfort food in a single pot. Gnocchi are small potato dumplings that can be interchanged with pasta. In this recipe, gnocchi, sausage, and kale cook in an easy, homemade tomato sauce.

1 pound mild Italian ground sausage

1 (28-ounce) can no-salt-added diced tomatoes

1 cup low-sodium beef broth

1 small onion, diced, or 1 tablespoon dried onion flakes

1 bell pepper, any color, seeded and diced

2 garlic cloves, minced

1 tablespoon Italian seasoning

1 teaspoon sea salt

½ teaspoon freshly ground black pepper

1 pound gnocchi

1 cup chopped kale

1. In a large skillet over medium-high heat, cook the sausage for 3 to 5 minutes, breaking it up with a spoon, until it has browned and is no longer pink. Drain the grease and put the cooked sausage in a slow cooker.

2. Add the tomatoes, beef broth, onion, bell pepper, garlic, Italian seasoning, salt, and black pepper to the sausage. Stir to mix well.

3. Cover the cooker and cook for 4 to 6 hours on Low heat.

4. Stir in the gnocchi and kale. Replace the cover on the cooker and cook for 15 to 30 minutes on Low heat, or until the gnocchi and kale are tender.

INGREDIENT TIP: Substitute your favorite dried herbs in place of the Italian seasoning blend, such as parsley, thyme, rosemary, marjoram, and basil.

Per Serving: Calories: 403; Total fat: 18g; Sodium: 1,565mg; Carbohydrates: 41g; Fiber: 5g; Sugar: 8g; Protein: 18g

MINESTRONE CASSEROLE WITH ITALIAN SAUSAGE

SERVES 4 // PREP TIME: 10 MINUTES // COOK TIME: 4 TO 6 HOURS ON LOW, PLUS 30 MINUTES ON LOW FOR THE MACARONI

Minestrone soup—but in casserole form! This dish uses all the ingredients of the typical minestrone that you love. Use a hot or mild Italian sausage, as you like; cut it into 1-inch pieces or use it ground and crumbled.

8 ounces Italian-style smoked sausage links, cut into 1-inch pieces

1 (28-ounce) can no-salt-added diced tomatoes

1 cup low-sodium vegetable broth

1 (15-ounce) can reduced-sodium chickpeas, drained and rinsed

3 celery stalks, diced

3 carrots, diced

1 onion, diced

4 garlic cloves, minced

8 ounces green beans, cut into 1-inch pieces

2 zucchini, diced

1 tablespoon Italian seasoning

1 teaspoon sea salt

½ teaspoon freshly ground black pepper

¼ teaspoon ground cumin

2 bay leaves

4 ounces elbow macaroni

⅓ cup grated Parmesan cheese

Fresh parsley, for garnish

1. In a slow cooker, combine the sausage, tomatoes, vegetable broth, chickpeas, celery, carrots, onion, garlic, green beans, zucchini, Italian seasoning, salt, pepper, cumin, and bay leaves. Stir to mix well.
2. Cover the cooker and cook for 4 to 6 hours on Low heat.
3. Remove and discard the bay leaves.
4. Stir in the macaroni and Parmesan cheese. Replace the cover on the cooker and cook for 30 minutes on Low heat, or until the macaroni is tender.
5. Garnish with fresh parsley for serving.

PREPARATION TIP: This is a great freezer meal recipe. In a 1-gallon-size, freezer-safe resealable bag that is double-bagged to prevent leaks, combine all of the ingredients raw except the pasta. Freeze for up to 2 months. Thaw overnight in the refrigerator the day before you are ready to cook. Add the ingredients to the slow cooker and follow the recipe as written, omitting the cheese in step 4 and parsley in step 5 as they are already included in your frozen ingredients.

Per Serving: Calories: 567; Total fat: 22g; Sodium: 1,428mg; Carbohydrates: 73g; Fiber: 17g; Sugar: 20g; Protein: 25g

TUNA NOODLE CASSEROLE

Tuna noodle casserole is an American classic, but this recipe adds your favorite Mediterranean vegetables for a unique twist. To make this a healthier dish, I used a combination of milk and broth instead of the usual processed cream-of-whatever soup.

Nonstick cooking spray

3 (5-ounce) cans tuna, drained

12 to 14 ounces dried egg noodles

2 cups low-sodium chicken broth

3 tablespoons unsalted butter

2 cups milk of your choice

¼ cup diced tomato

¼ cup diced red onion

¼ cup sliced mushrooms

¼ cup diced zucchini

1 small bell pepper, any color, seeded and diced

1½ cups shredded mozzarella cheese

2 teaspoons dried parsley

2 teaspoons sea salt

½ teaspoon freshly ground black pepper

½ cup crumbled feta cheese

1. Generously coat a slow-cooker insert with cooking spray.
2. In a large bowl, stir together the tuna, noodles, chicken broth, butter, milk, tomato, onion, mushrooms, zucchini, bell pepper, mozzarella cheese, parsley, salt, and black pepper. Pour the tuna mixture into the prepared slow cooker.
3. Cover the cooker and cook for 4 to 6 hours on Low heat.
4. Top with the feta cheese for serving.

VARIATION TIP: For a more protein-heavy meal, add an additional can of tuna and follow the recipe as written.

Per Serving: Calories: 482; Total fat: 18g; Sodium: 1,346mg; Carbohydrates: 49g; Fiber: 4g; Sugar: 7g; Protein: 33g

CREAMY CHICKEN PASTA

SERVES 4 // PREP TIME: 10 MINUTES // COOK TIME: 4 TO 6 HOURS ON LOW,
PLUS 15 TO 30 MINUTES ON LOW FOR THE PASTA

This kid-friendly chicken pasta recipe is creamy and flavorful, yet simple. Use your favorite shape of pasta, like penne, fettuccine, spaghetti, or linguine. You can even use quinoa or brown rice pasta to make this recipe gluten-free.

¼ cup water

2 tablespoons arrowroot flour

2 pounds boneless, skinless chicken breasts or thighs

1 (28-ounce) can no-salt-added diced tomatoes, plus more as needed

1 green or red bell pepper, seeded and diced

1 small red onion, diced

2 garlic cloves, minced

1 teaspoon dried oregano

1 teaspoon dried parsley

1 teaspoon sea salt

½ teaspoon freshly ground black pepper

8 ounces dried pasta

1 cup low-sodium chicken broth (optional)

1. In a small bowl, whisk together the water and arrowroot flour until the flour dissolves.
2. In a slow cooker, combine the chicken, tomatoes, bell pepper, onion, garlic, oregano, parsley, salt, black pepper, and arrowroot mixture. Stir to mix well.
3. Cover the cooker and cook for 4 to 6 hours on Low heat.
4. Stir in the pasta, making sure it is completely submerged. If it is not, add an additional 1 cup of diced tomatoes or 1 cup of chicken broth. Replace the cover on the cooker and cook for 15 to 30 minutes on Low heat, or until the pasta is tender.

INGREDIENT TIP: In place of the arrowroot flour, use your preferred thickening agent such as cornstarch, potato starch, etc.

Per Serving: Calories: 497; Total fat: 6g; Sodium: 1,031mg; Carbohydrates: 60g; Fiber: 7g; Sugar: 10g; Protein: 55g

GREEK CHICKEN PASTA CASSEROLE

SERVES 4 // PREP TIME: 15 MINUTES // COOK TIME: 4 TO 6 HOURS ON LOW

Greek pasta salad is a light dish that is popular for picnics and potlucks. I took the essence of a Greek pasta salad, added chicken, and converted it into a slow-cooker recipe. Garnish this casserole with your favorite pasta salad ingredients like fresh diced cucumber.

2 pounds boneless, skinless chicken thighs or breasts, cut into 1-inch pieces

8 ounces dried rotini pasta

7 cups low-sodium chicken broth

½ red onion, diced

3 garlic cloves, minced

¼ cup whole Kalamata olives, pitted

3 Roma tomatoes, diced

2 tablespoons red wine vinegar

1 teaspoon extra-virgin olive oil

2 teaspoons dried oregano

1 teaspoon sea salt

½ teaspoon freshly ground black pepper

¼ cup crumbled feta cheese

1. In a slow cooker, combine the chicken, pasta, chicken broth, onion, garlic, olives, tomatoes, vinegar, olive oil, oregano, salt, and pepper. Stir to mix well.

2. Cover the cooker and cook for 4 to 6 hours on Low heat.

3. Garnish with the feta cheese for serving.

VARIATION TIP: Love tomatoes? Make this a tomato-based casserole by using no-salt-added crushed or diced tomatoes instead of the broth. Or, make this a vegetarian casserole using 4 additional cups of chopped vegetables in place of the chicken, and vegetable broth instead of the chicken broth.

Per Serving: Calories: 559; Total fat: 22g; Sodium: 1,253mg; Carbohydrates: 50g; Fiber: 7g; Sugar: 8g; Protein: 46g

RIGATONI WITH LAMB MEATBALLS

SERVES 4 // PREP TIME: 15 MINUTES // COOK TIME: 3 TO 5 HOURS ON LOW

Similar to a Bolognese sauce, flavorful lamb meatballs simmer in a tomato sauce along with rigatoni in this hearty pasta dish. Don't like lamb? Use ground beef in its place. Serve this meal with a simple salad or your favorite green vegetable on the side.

8 ounces dried rigatoni pasta

2 (28-ounce) cans no-salt-added crushed tomatoes or no-salt-added diced tomatoes

1 small onion, diced

1 bell pepper, any color, seeded and diced

3 garlic cloves, minced, divided

1 pound raw ground lamb

1 large egg

2 tablespoons bread crumbs

1 tablespoon dried parsley

1 teaspoon dried oregano

1 teaspoon sea salt

½ teaspoon freshly ground black pepper

1. In a slow cooker, combine the pasta, tomatoes, onion, bell pepper, and 1 clove of garlic. Stir to mix well.

2. In a large bowl, mix together the ground lamb, egg, bread crumbs, the remaining 2 garlic cloves, parsley, oregano, salt, and black pepper until all of the ingredients are evenly blended. Shape the meat mixture into 6 to 9 large meatballs. Nestle the meatballs into the pasta and tomato sauce.

3. Cover the cooker and cook for 3 to 5 hours on Low heat, or until the pasta is tender.

PREPARATION TIP: Garnish with fresh chopped parsley and a sprinkle of Parmesan cheese if desired.

Per Serving: Calories: 653; Total fat: 29g; Sodium: 847mg; Carbohydrates: 69g; Fiber: 10g; Sugar: 17g; Protein: 32g

VEGETABLES

EGGPLANT "LASAGNA"

SERVES 6 // PREP TIME: 10 MINUTES // COOK TIME: 6 TO 8 HOURS ON LOW

Eggplant replaces pasta in this low-carb version of a classic Italian recipe. You can use your favorite cheese combination—it does not have to be cottage cheese and ricotta. Just remember to place the layers of food in the slow cooker in the following order: tomatoes, eggplant, vegetables, and cheese.

2 medium globe eggplants, peeled and thinly sliced to resemble lasagna noodles

1 teaspoon sea salt, plus more for the eggplant

2 cups cottage cheese

½ cup ricotta

1 large egg

½ teaspoon freshly ground black pepper

1 (28-ounce) can no-salt-added diced tomatoes

1 small onion, diced

1 bell pepper, any color, seeded and diced

4 ounces mushrooms, sliced

1. Lay the eggplant slices on paper towels in a single layer and lightly sprinkle them with salt. Let them sit for 10 to 30 minutes to draw out excess moisture.

2. In a medium bowl, stir together the cottage cheese, ricotta, egg, the remaining 1 teaspoon of salt, and black pepper.

3. Cover the bottom of a slow cooker with one-quarter of the tomatoes.

4. Blot the eggplant slices with a paper towel to remove the excess liquid and salt.

5. Layer one-quarter each of the eggplant, onion, bell pepper, mushrooms, and cottage cheese mixture. Repeat the layers in the same sequence until all of the ingredients are used.

6. Cover the cooker and cook for 6 to 8 hours on Low heat.

7. Let cool slightly before slicing and serving.

VARIATION TIP: This does not have to be a vegetarian dish. Layer in up to 1 pound of cooked ground meat to make this lasagna a heartier meal.

Per Serving: Calories: 204; Total fat: 7g; Sodium: 781mg; Carbohydrates: 23g; Fiber: 7g; Sugar: 14g; Protein: 15g

EGG CASSEROLE WITH TOMATO, SPINACH, AND FETA

SERVES 6 // PREP TIME: 10 MINUTES // COOK TIME: 6 TO 8 HOURS ON LOW

Personally, I think eggs can be eaten during any time of the day, but I understand that may not be the case for everyone. This egg casserole is a great addition to your next brunch menu or your daily breakfast.

12 large eggs

¼ cup milk of your choice

1 cup fresh spinach, chopped

¼ cup feta cheese, crumbled

½ teaspoon sea salt

¼ teaspoon freshly ground black pepper

Nonstick cooking spray

2 Roma tomatoes, sliced

1. In a medium bowl, whisk together the eggs, milk, spinach, feta cheese, salt, and pepper until combined.
2. Generously coat a slow-cooker insert with cooking spray.
3. Pour the egg mixture into the slow cooker. Top with the tomato slices.
4. Cover the cooker and cook for 6 to 8 hours on Low heat.

INGREDIENT TIP: If you have other vegetables on hand, like diced onion, bell pepper, or mushrooms, add them too.

Per Serving: Calories: 178; Total fat: 11g; Sodium: 416mg; Carbohydrates: 4g; Fiber: 1g; Sugar: 3g; Protein: 14g

VEGETABLE TERRINE

SERVES 6 // PREP TIME: 30 MINUTES // COOK TIME: 5 TO 7 HOURS ON LOW

A vegetable terrine is a mix of vegetables that has been cooked, cooled, and then served in slices. The key to this Mediterranean version is to stack the vegetables in the slow cooker and, after cooking, let them cool completely before slicing. This recipe is a bit more labor-intensive because of all the slicing and layering of the vegetables, but the flavorful, satisfying result is worth it.

PREPARATION TIP: For extra flavor, roast the vegetables on the grill or under the broiler until their skins blacken; then peel off the skins before adding the vegetables to the slow cooker.

---

1 small eggplant, thinly sliced lengthwise

2 green bell peppers, halved, seeded, and sliced

2 red bell peppers, halved, seeded, and sliced

1 portobello mushroom, cut into ¼-inch-thick slices

1 zucchini, thinly sliced lengthwise

1 large red onion, cut into ¼-inch-thick rounds

2 yellow squash, thinly sliced lengthwise

4 large tomatoes, sliced

1 teaspoon sea salt

¼ teaspoon freshly ground black pepper

Nonstick cooking spray

1 cup grated Parmesan cheese

2 tablespoons extra-virgin olive oil

1 tablespoon red wine vinegar

2 teaspoons freshly squeezed lemon juice

1 teaspoon dried basil

1 garlic clove, minced

1. Season the eggplant, green and red bell peppers, mushroom, zucchini, onion, squash, and tomatoes with salt and black pepper, but keep all the vegetables separate.

2. Generously coat a slow-cooker insert with cooking spray, or line the bottom and sides with parchment paper or aluminum foil.

3. Starting with half of the eggplant, line the bottom of the prepared slow cooker with overlapping slices. Sprinkle with 2 tablespoons of Parmesan cheese.

4. Add a second layer using half of the green and red bell peppers. Sprinkle with 2 more tablespoons of Parmesan cheese.

5. Add a third layer using half of the mushroom slices. Sprinkle with 2 more tablespoons of Parmesan cheese.

6. Add a fourth layer using half of the zucchini slices. Sprinkle with 2 more tablespoons of Parmesan cheese.

7. Add a fifth layer using half of the red onion slices. Sprinkle with another 2 tablespoons of Parmesan cheese.

8. Add a sixth layer using half of the yellow squash slices. Sprinkle with 2 more tablespoons of Parmesan cheese.

9. Add a final seventh layer with half of the tomato slices. Sprinkle with 2 more tablespoons of Parmesan cheese.

10. Repeat the layering with the remaining vegetables and Parmesan cheese in the same order until all of the vegetables have been used.

11. In a small bowl, whisk together the olive oil, vinegar, lemon juice, basil, and garlic until combined. Pour the mixture over the vegetables. Top with any remaining Parmesan cheese.

12. Cover the cooker and cook for 5 to 7 hours on Low heat.

13. Let cool to room temperature before slicing and serving.

Per Serving: Calories: 217; Total fat: 11g; Sodium: 725mg; Carbohydrates: 24g; Fiber: 7g; Sugar: 8g; Protein: 12g

BABA GHANOUSH

Baba ghanoush is a Lebanese dip consisting of eggplant, tahini (a sesame seed paste), olive oil, lemon juice, and seasonings. The eggplant is usually baked or broiled, but here it is cooked in the slow cooker along with the other ingredients. Serve this baba ghanoush with crackers, pita, or even veggie sticks. Although it is traditionally served as an appetizer, it can also be used as a hearty, savory spread on sandwiches.

1 large eggplant (2 to 4 pounds), peeled and diced

¼ cup freshly squeezed lemon juice

2 garlic cloves, minced

2 tablespoons tahini

1 teaspoon extra-virgin olive oil, plus more as needed

¼ teaspoon sea salt, plus more as needed

⅛ teaspoon freshly ground black pepper, plus more as needed

2 tablespoons chopped fresh parsley

1. In a slow cooker, combine the eggplant, lemon juice, garlic, tahini, olive oil, salt, and pepper. Stir to mix well.
2. Cover the cooker and cook for 2 to 4 hours on Low heat.
3. Using a spoon or potato masher, mash the mixture. If you prefer a smoother texture, transfer it to a food processor and blend to your desired consistency. Taste and season with olive oil, salt, and pepper as needed.
4. Garnish with fresh parsley for serving.

PREPARATION TIP: If you have time, broil the peeled, diced eggplant for 5 to 10 minutes, or until it turns soft and golden brown, before adding it to the slow cooker. This gives it a smoky flavor.

Per Serving: Calories: 81; Total fat: 4g; Sodium: 108mg; Carbohydrates: 12g; Fiber: 4g; Sugar: 6g; Protein: 3g

STEAMED VEGETABLES

SERVES 6 // PREP TIME: 10 MINUTES // COOK TIME: 5 TO 7 HOURS ON LOW

Vegetables of all sorts, shapes, sizes, colors, and flavors are a focus of the Mediterranean diet. This recipe—one of the easiest in this cookbook—offers a customizable way to easily add more tasty veggies to your plate at any meal. No fancy techniques or ingredients are required—all you need are your favorite vegetables (any that you like, even potatoes), a few seasonings, and a drizzle of olive oil. No other liquid is needed. That is right—you do not add any liquid to the recipe. But you do get lots of delicious, healthy veggies in the end.

2 pounds fresh vegetables of your choice, sliced

1 teaspoon dried thyme

1 teaspoon dried rosemary

1 teaspoon sea salt

¼ teaspoon freshly ground black pepper

2 tablespoons extra-virgin olive oil

1. Put the vegetables in a slow cooker and season them with thyme, rosemary, salt, and pepper.
2. Drizzle the olive oil on top.
3. Cover the cooker and cook for 5 to 7 hours on Low heat, or until the vegetables are tender.

VARIATION TIP: In addition to your favorite vegetables, use your favorite herbs, too, substituting others for the thyme and rosemary. Fresh herbs also work well in this recipe.

Per Serving: Calories: 85; Total fat: 5g; Sodium: 442mg; Carbohydrates: 11g; Fiber: 3g; Sugar: 5g; Protein: 1g

STUFFED ARTICHOKES

SERVES 4 TO 6 // PREP TIME: 20 MINUTES // COOK TIME: 5 TO 7 HOURS ON LOW

Stuffed artichokes are popular in many Mediterranean countries, and each country has its own version of the dish. This slow-cooker version is made without meat. The number of artichokes you use will depend on how large your slow cooker is. If you have a 5- to 6-quart cooker, you should be able to fit 4 to 6 large artichokes in it.

4 to 6 fresh large artichokes

½ cup bread crumbs

½ cup grated Parmesan cheese or Romano cheese

4 garlic cloves, minced

½ teaspoon sea salt

½ teaspoon freshly ground black pepper

¼ cup water

2 tablespoons extra-virgin olive oil

2 tablespoons chopped fresh parsley for garnish (optional)

1. To trim and prepare the artichokes, cut off the bottom along with 1 inch from the top of each artichoke. Pull off and discard the lowest leaves nearest the stem end. Trim off any pointy tips of artichoke leaves that are poking out. Set aside.
2. In a small bowl, stir together the bread crumbs, Parmesan cheese, garlic, salt, and pepper.
3. Spread apart the artichoke leaves and stuff the bread-crumb mixture into the spaces, down to the base.
4. Pour the water into a slow cooker.
5. Place the artichokes in the slow cooker in a single layer. Drizzle the olive oil over the artichokes.
6. Cover the cooker and cook for 5 to 7 hours on Low heat, or until the artichokes are tender.
7. Garnish with fresh parsley if desired.

VARIATION TIP: Add 1 tablespoon of dried herbs such as parsley, oregano, or thyme to the bread-crumb mixture. Make this a nonvegetarian recipe by adding 8 ounces of cooked meat or poultry to the stuffing.

Per Serving: Calories: 224; Total fat: 12g; Sodium: 883mg; Carbohydrates: 23g; Fiber: 8g; Sugar: 2g; Protein: 12g

ZUCCHINI PARMESAN CASSEROLE

SERVES 4 // PREP TIME: 10 MINUTES // COOK TIME: 5 TO 7 HOURS ON LOW

Serve this casserole as a side dish with your weeknight dinner or as a main dish to impress your vegetarian friends. Add more cheese if you like; Romano cheese can be mixed in with the Parmesan cheese.

1 (15-ounce) can no-salt-added diced tomatoes

6 zucchini, cut into ¼-inch-thick rounds

2 tablespoons unsalted butter, melted

1 small onion, chopped

2 garlic cloves, minced

1 teaspoon garlic powder

1 teaspoon dried oregano

1 teaspoon sea salt

½ teaspoon dried basil

¼ teaspoon freshly ground black pepper

1 cup grated Parmesan cheese

1. Put the tomatoes in a slow cooker.
2. In a large bowl, stir together the zucchini, melted butter, onion, garlic, garlic powder, oregano, salt, basil, and pepper. Pour the zucchini mixture over the tomatoes.
3. Spread the Parmesan cheese on top of the zucchini mixture.
4. Cover the cooker and cook for 5 to 7 hours on Low heat.

INGREDIENT TIP: To make this a more colorful dish, use 3 zucchini and 3 yellow squash.

Per Serving: Calories: 247; Total fat: 14g; Sodium: 1,123mg; Carbohydrates: 19g; Fiber: 6g; Sugar: 9g; Protein: 16g

MEDITERRANEAN RATATOUILLE

SERVES 6 // PREP TIME: 10 MINUTES // COOK TIME: 5 TO 7 HOURS ON LOW

Ratatouille is a French vegetable dish that you can adapt any way you like using your favorite ingredients. This version uses Mediterranean vegetables and seasonings.

1 (15-ounce) can no-salt-added diced tomatoes

2 zucchini, chopped

1 small eggplant, peeled and cubed

1 green or red bell pepper, seeded and chopped

1 small onion, chopped

3 garlic cloves, minced

1 tablespoon extra-virgin olive oil

1 tablespoon red wine vinegar

1 teaspoon sea salt

1 teaspoon dried thyme

1 teaspoon dried oregano

1 teaspoon smoked paprika

½ teaspoon freshly ground black pepper

¼ cup chopped fresh basil

1. In a slow cooker, combine the tomatoes, zucchini, eggplant, bell pepper, onion, garlic, olive oil, vinegar, salt, thyme, oregano, paprika, and black pepper. Stir to mix well.

2. Cover the cooker and cook for 5 to 7 hours on Low heat.

3. Garnish with fresh basil for serving.

VARIATION TIP: Make this a ratatouille stew by adding 2 cups of low-sodium vegetable broth.

Per Serving: Calories: 80; Total fat: 3g; Sodium: 427mg; Carbohydrates: 14g; Fiber: 5g; Sugar: 7g; Protein: 3g

POTATO VEGETABLE HASH

SERVES 4 // PREP TIME: 20 MINUTES // COOK TIME: 5 TO 7 HOURS ON LOW

Combining potatoes and vegetables is a great way to create a hearty, vegetarian one-pot recipe. You can serve this hash at any time of the day. If you want to use a different kind of potato other than red, keep in mind that waxy potatoes work best with slow cooking because they hold their shape better during the long cook time.

1½ pounds red potatoes, diced

8 ounces green beans, trimmed and cut into ½-inch pieces

4 ounces mushrooms, chopped

1 large tomato, chopped

1 large zucchini, diced

1 small onion, diced

1 red bell pepper, seeded and chopped

⅓ cup low-sodium vegetable broth

1 teaspoon sea salt

½ teaspoon garlic powder

½ teaspoon freshly ground black pepper

¼ teaspoon red pepper flakes

¼ cup shredded cheese of your choice (optional)

1. In a slow cooker, combine the potatoes, green beans, mushrooms, tomato, zucchini, onion, bell pepper, vegetable broth, salt, garlic powder, black pepper, and red pepper flakes. Stir to mix well.
2. Cover the cooker and cook for 5 to 7 hours on Low heat.
3. Garnish with cheese for serving (if using).

VARIATION TIP: To serve this as a breakfast hash: Once it is done cooking, add some cooked eggs on top (1 to 2 per person).

Per Serving: Calories: 183; Total fat: 1g; Sodium: 642mg; Carbohydrates: 41g; Fiber: 8g; Sugar: 8g; Protein: 7g

GREEK FASOLAKIA (GREEN BEANS)

SERVES 6 // PREP TIME: 10 MINUTES // COOK TIME: 6 TO 8 HOURS ON LOW

Fasolakia are green beans. Although this is a simple dish, it is full of flavor. In Greece, these green beans are served as a main dish with bread. They can also be served as a side dish since they pair nicely with grilled fish, chicken, or lamb.

2 pounds green beans, trimmed

1 (15-ounce) can no-salt-added diced tomatoes, with juice

1 large onion, chopped

4 garlic cloves, chopped

Juice of 1 lemon

1 teaspoon dried dill

1 teaspoon ground cumin

1 teaspoon dried oregano

1 teaspoon sea salt

½ teaspoon freshly ground black pepper

¼ cup feta cheese, crumbled

1. In a slow cooker, combine the green beans, tomatoes and their juice, onion, garlic, lemon juice, dill, cumin, oregano, salt, and pepper. Stir to mix well.
2. Cover the cooker and cook for 6 to 8 hours on Low heat.
3. Top with feta cheese for serving.

INGREDIENT TIP: Frozen green beans can be used in this recipe in place of fresh. No need to thaw them—just add them to the slow cooker directly from the freezer.

Per Serving: Calories: 94; Total fat: 2g; Sodium: 497mg; Carbohydrates: 18g; Fiber: 7g; Sugar: 9g; Protein: 5g

Paella,
page 76

SEAFOOD

MOROCCAN FISH

SERVES 4 // PREP TIME: 10 MINUTES // COOK TIME: 2 TO 4 HOURS ON LOW

Moroccan flavors slow-cook with your favorite fish in this aromatic and flavorful seafood recipe. A store-bought *ras al-hanout* seasoning blend (2 teaspoons) can be used instead of the homemade spice mix given here. This dish is delicious served over cooked rice.

FOR THE RAS AL-HANOUT

¼ teaspoon ground cumin

¼ teaspoon ground ginger

¼ teaspoon ground turmeric

¼ teaspoon paprika

¼ teaspoon garlic powder

¼ teaspoon red pepper flakes

⅛ teaspoon ground cinnamon

⅛ teaspoon ground coriander

⅛ teaspoon ground nutmeg

⅛ teaspoon ground cloves

⅛ teaspoon sea salt

⅛ teaspoon freshly ground black pepper

FOR THE FISH

Nonstick cooking spray

2 pounds fresh white-fleshed fish fillets of your choice

2 garlic cloves, minced

TO MAKE THE RAS AL-HANOUT

In a small bowl, stir together the cumin, ginger, turmeric, paprika, garlic powder, red pepper flakes, cinnamon, coriander, nutmeg, cloves, salt, and pepper.

TO MAKE THE FISH

1. Coat a slow-cooker insert with cooking spray, or line the bottom and sides with parchment paper or aluminum foil.

2. Season the fish all over with the ras al-hanout and garlic. Place the fish in the prepared slow cooker in a single layer, cutting it into pieces to fit if needed.

3. Cover the cooker and cook for 2 to 4 hours on Low heat.

VARIATION TIP: Make this a fish stew by adding 2 cups of low-sodium vegetable broth or low-sodium chicken broth. If you do so, skip step 1 of the recipe.

INGREDIENT TIP: Substitute frozen fish for fresh. Fish with dense flesh (like halibut and tuna) can be cooked directly from a frozen state, but delicate fish like cod or sole need to be thawed first.

Per Serving: Calories: 243; Total fat: 2g; Sodium: 216mg; Carbohydrates: 1g; Fiber: <1g; Sugar: 0g; Protein: 51g

HALIBUT WITH LEMON AND CAPERS

SERVES 4 // PREP TIME: 10 MINUTES // COOK TIME: 2 TO 4 HOURS ON LOW

This recipe features flavors of the popular Italian dish chicken piccata. I use halibut instead of chicken because the lemon and capers perfectly complement this fish. Of course, you can substitute a comparable white-fleshed fish in place of the halibut.

Nonstick cooking spray

2 pounds fresh halibut fillets

1 teaspoon extra-virgin olive oil

2 garlic cloves, minced

1 tablespoon dried parsley

½ teaspoon sea salt

⅛ teaspoon freshly ground black pepper

¼ cup freshly squeezed lemon juice

¼ cup drained capers

2 lemons, thinly sliced

1. Coat a slow-cooker insert with cooking spray or line the bottom and sides with parchment paper or aluminum foil.
2. Rub the halibut all over with the olive oil. Season the fish with garlic, parsley, salt, and pepper. Place the fish in the prepared slow cooker in a single layer, cutting it into pieces to fit if needed.
3. Pour the lemon juice and capers on top of the halibut. Top the fish with lemon slices.
4. Cover the cooker and cook for 2 to 4 hours on Low heat.

SERVING TIP: Serve this citrusy dish over cooked rice or with a side of roasted potatoes.

Per Serving: Calories: 347; Total fat: 8g; Sodium: 706mg; Carbohydrates: 8g; Fiber: 3g; Sugar: 1g; Protein: 62g

PAELLA

Originating from Valencia, Spain, paella is a traditional dish that can be made in many ways. On the Mediterranean coast, seafood is often used instead of the original meat and green beans. This version uses a combination of chicken, sausage, and your favorite seafood.

1½ cups raw long-grain brown rice

3 cups low-sodium chicken broth

1 (15-ounce) can no-salt-added diced tomatoes

8 ounces smoked sausage, cut into 1-inch-thick rounds

1 small onion, diced

¼ cup peas (raw, frozen, or canned)

2 garlic cloves, minced

1 tablespoon extra-virgin olive oil

1½ teaspoons paprika

1 teaspoon sea salt

½ teaspoon freshly ground black pepper

½ teaspoon ground turmeric

8 ounces boneless, skinless chicken thighs, cut into 1-inch pieces

4 ounces mussels, rinsed with cold water (optional)

1½ pounds whole raw medium shrimp, peeled and deveined

1. In a slow cooker, combine the rice, chicken broth, tomatoes, smoked sausage, onion, peas, garlic, olive oil, paprika, salt, pepper, and turmeric. Stir to mix well.

2. Place the chicken thighs on top of the ingredients in the cooker.

3. Cover the cooker and cook for 6 to 8 hours on Low heat.

4. Use your hands to rub off any debris from the mussel shells (if using). Add the shrimp and mussels in their shells to the slow cooker. Replace the cover on the cooker and cook for 15 to 30 minutes on Low heat, or until the shrimp have turned pink and the mussels have opened their shells. Discard any mussels that remain closed.

INGREDIENT TIP: Use your favorite seafood in this dish—whether it is fish or even clams. You can also use frozen raw shrimp, but thaw them first.

Per Serving: Calories: 678; Total fat: 26g; Sodium: 909mg; Carbohydrates: 67g; Fiber: 6g; Sugar: 6g; Protein: 51g

SEASONED SOLE

SERVES 4 // PREP TIME: 5 MINUTES // COOK TIME: 2 TO 4 HOURS ON LOW

The name of this recipe is "Seasoned Sole" for a reason. It might not be obvious from the ingredient list, but the character of these seasonings really emerges while this dish slow-cooks.

Nonstick cooking spray

2 pounds fresh sole fillets

3 tablespoons freshly squeezed lime juice

2 tablespoons extra-virgin olive oil

2 garlic cloves, minced

1 tablespoon ground cumin

1½ teaspoons paprika

1 teaspoon sea salt

¼ cup fresh cilantro

1. Coat a slow-cooker insert with cooking spray, or line the bottom and sides with parchment paper or aluminum foil.
2. Place the sole in the prepared slow cooker in a single layer, cutting it into pieces to fit if needed.
3. In a small bowl, whisk together the lime juice, olive oil, garlic, cumin, paprika, and salt until blended. Pour the sauce over the fish.
4. Cover the cooker and cook for 2 to 4 hours on Low heat.
5. Garnish with fresh cilantro for serving.

INGREDIENT TIP: If you prefer, use another white-fleshed fish, such as halibut, cod, tilapia, or haddock.

Per Serving: Calories: 234; Total fat: 12g; Sodium: 713mg; Carbohydrates: 2g; Fiber: 1g; Sugar: 1g; Protein: 29g

CIOPPINO

Cioppino is an Italian-American fish stew. This version uses fish stock instead of the traditional white wine. If you cannot get fish stock, use low-sodium vegetable stock or water.

1 (28-ounce) can no-salt-added diced tomatoes

2 cups low-sodium fish stock

1 (6-ounce) can no-salt-added tomato sauce

2 celery stalks, diced

1 onion, diced

1 bell pepper, any color, seeded and diced

4 garlic cloves, minced

2 teaspoons Italian seasoning

½ teaspoon sea salt

½ teaspoon red pepper flakes

1 bay leaf

1 tablespoon extra-virgin olive oil

1 pound fresh fish fillets of your choice, cut into 1-inch pieces

8 ounces mussels, rinsed in cold water

8 ounces whole raw medium shrimp, peeled and deveined

8 ounces scallops

Fresh parsley, for garnish (optional)

1. In a slow cooker, combine the tomatoes, fish stock, tomato sauce, celery, onion, bell pepper, garlic, Italian seasoning, salt, red pepper flakes, bay leaf, and olive oil. Stir to mix well.

2. Cover the cooker and cook for 4 to 6 hours on Low heat.

3. Use your hands to rub off any debris from the mussel shells. Add the fish, mussels in their shells, shrimp, and scallops to the cioppino. Replace the cover on the cooker and cook for 30 minutes on Low heat.

4. Remove and discard the bay leaf and any mussels that remain closed.

5. Top with fresh parsley (if using) for serving.

INGREDIENT TIP: Use any combination of your favorite seafood—whether it includes fish, mussels, shrimp, crab, scallops, clams, or other shellfish. You can also use frozen raw seafood—but thaw it first, unless it's a very sturdy fish like halibut. You can use any fish in this recipe; I tend to use cod.

Per Serving: Calories: 285; Total fat: 5g; Sodium: 617mg; Carbohydrates: 18g; Fiber: 4g; Sugar: 8g; Protein: 41g

TOMATO-BASIL SALMON

SERVES 4 // PREP TIME: 10 MINUTES // COOK TIME: 4 TO 6 HOURS ON LOW

This simple salmon recipe uses just a few ingredients, but you would never know it by the taste. This recipe produces about 2 cups of tasty tomato sauce. Serve this dish with pita or a hearty bread to dip into the sauce.

1 (15-ounce) can no-salt-added crushed tomatoes

½ cup chopped onion

4 teaspoons dried basil

3 garlic cloves, minced

2 pounds fresh salmon fillets, skin on or off as preferred

1 teaspoon sea salt

¼ teaspoon freshly ground black pepper

¼ cup chopped fresh basil

1. In a slow cooker, combine the tomatoes, onion, basil, and garlic. Stir to mix well.

2. Season the salmon all over with salt and pepper. Add the salmon to the slow cooker, cutting it into pieces to fit if needed, and spoon some of the tomato mixture on top.

3. Cover the cooker and cook for 4 to 6 hours on Low heat.

4. Garnish with fresh basil for serving.

SERVING TIP: Topping this tomato-basil salmon with fresh mozzarella cheese will give it the look and flavor of an Italian caprese salad.

Per Serving: Calories: 471; Total fat: 24g; Sodium: 733mg; Carbohydrates: 9g; Fiber: 3g; Sugar: 4g; Protein: 58g

FISH CHILI

SERVES 6 // PREP TIME: 10 MINUTES // COOK TIME: 5 TO 7 HOURS ON LOW, PLUS 30 MINUTES ON LOW FOR THE FISH

This seafood twist on a classic chili uses lots of seafood, vegetables, and familiar chili seasonings. This is yet another recipe in which you can use whatever fish you like—whether it is salmon, halibut, or cod (my personal favorite). Note that fish with dense flesh (like salmon, halibut, and tuna) can be cooked directly from a frozen state, but delicate fish like cod or sole need to be thawed first before putting in the slow cooker.

1 (28-ounce) can no-salt-added diced tomatoes

1 (15-ounce) can reduced sodium white beans, drained and rinsed

1 (10-ounce) can no-salt-added diced tomatoes with green chiles

1 (8-ounce) can no-salt-added tomato sauce

3 garlic cloves, minced

1 small onion, diced

1 bell pepper, any color, seeded and diced

2 tablespoons chili powder

2 teaspoons ground cumin

1½ teaspoons paprika

1 teaspoon sea salt

1 teaspoon dried oregano

2 pounds fresh or frozen fish fillets of your choice, cut into 2-inch pieces

1. In a slow cooker, combine the tomatoes, beans, tomatoes with green chiles, tomato sauce, garlic, onion, bell pepper, chili powder, cumin, paprika, salt, and oregano. Stir to mix well.

2. Cover the cooker and cook for 5 to 7 hours on Low heat.

3. Stir in the fish, replace the cover on the cooker, and cook for 30 minutes on Low heat.

VARIATION TIP: Make this a spicy chili by adding 1 teaspoon of red pepper flakes in step 1.

Per Serving: Calories: 292; Total fat: 2g; Sodium: 611mg; Carbohydrates: 27g; Fiber: 9g; Sugar: 9g; Protein: 41g

SESAME-GINGER COD

Switch things up a bit while still getting your recommended fish intake with this Asian-inspired sesame-ginger recipe. With Mediterranean staples like balsamic vinegar, olive oil, and lemon juice, this dish combines simple ingredients from both cuisines. Save the sauce; it is delectable for dipping bread into.

¼ cup low-sodium soy sauce

2 tablespoons balsamic vinegar

1 tablespoon freshly squeezed lemon juice

2 teaspoons extra-virgin olive oil

1 tablespoon ground ginger

½ teaspoon sea salt

¼ teaspoon freshly ground black pepper

Nonstick cooking spray

2 pounds fresh cod fillets

½ teaspoon sesame seeds

4 scallions, green parts only, cut into 3-inch lengths

1. In a small bowl, whisk together the soy sauce, vinegar, lemon juice, olive oil, ginger, salt, and pepper until combined. Set aside.

2. Coat a slow-cooker insert with cooking spray and place the cod in the prepared slow cooker. Pour the soy sauce mixture over the cod.

3. Cover the cooker and cook for 4 to 6 hours on Low heat.

4. Garnish with sesame seeds and scallions for serving.

PREPARATION TIP: If you prefer a thicker sauce, stir 1 tablespoon of flour or starch into 2 tablespoons of water until dissolved. Stir this mixture into the slow cooker and cook for 5 to 10 minutes on Low heat, or until the sauce has thickened to your liking.

Per Serving: Calories: 282; Total fat: 4g; Sodium: 1,048mg; Carbohydrates: 4g; Fiber: 1g; Sugar: <1g; Protein: 52g

SHRIMP RISOTTO

SERVES 4 // PREP TIME: 10 MINUTES // COOK TIME: 4 TO 6 HOURS ON LOW,
PLUS 15 TO 30 MINUTES ON LOW FOR THE SHRIMP

This easy risotto uses arborio rice, which is a short-grain rice typically used for risottos. This rice is known for absorbing liquid without becoming mushy. If you do not like shrimp or want to try something different, substitute frozen (but thawed) langostinos.

1½ cups raw arborio rice

4½ cups low-sodium chicken broth

½ cup diced onion

2 garlic cloves, minced

½ teaspoon sea salt

½ teaspoon dried parsley

¼ teaspoon freshly ground black pepper

1 pound whole raw medium shrimp, peeled and deveined

¼ cup grated Parmesan cheese

1. In a slow cooker, combine the rice, chicken broth, onion, garlic, salt, parsley, and pepper. Stir to mix well.
2. Cover the cooker and cook for 4 to 6 hours on Low heat.
3. Stir in the shrimp and Parmesan cheese. Replace the cover on the cooker and cook for 15 to 30 minutes on Low heat, or until the shrimp have turned pink and the cheese is melted.

INGREDIENT TIP: If you cannot find arborio rice, use a long-grain brown rice instead, as it holds up best during the long cook time. You can also use frozen shrimp, but thaw them first.

Per Serving: Calories: 376; Total fat: 3g; Sodium: 602mg; Carbohydrates: 59g; Fiber: 1g; Sugar: 1g; Protein: 28g

SHRIMP FOIL PACKETS

SERVES 4 // PREP TIME: 15 MINUTES // COOK TIME: 4 TO 6 HOURS ON LOW

Shrimp, salmon, white-fleshed fish, or even a combination of these all work in this easy slow-cooker recipe. Using aluminum foil in the slow cooker (yes, you can use foil!) locks in the flavor and makes cleanup easy. You will need 2 sheets of foil (about 20 inches each) for each of the 4 foil packets.

1½ pounds whole raw medium shrimp, peeled, deveined, and divided into 4 (6-ounce) portions

Sea salt

Freshly ground black pepper

2 teaspoons extra-virgin olive oil, divided

4 teaspoons balsamic vinegar, divided

4 garlic cloves, minced

1 red onion, cut into chunks

1 large zucchini, sliced

4 Roma tomatoes, chopped

4 teaspoons dried oregano, divided

Juice of 1 lemon

1. Place a large sheet of aluminum foil on a work surface. Lay one-quarter of the shrimp in the center of the foil and season it with salt and pepper. Drizzle with ½ teaspoon of olive oil and 1 teaspoon of vinegar.

2. Top the shrimp with one-quarter each of the garlic, onion, and zucchini, plus 1 tomato and 1 teaspoon of oregano. Place a second sheet of foil on top of the ingredients. Fold the corners over to seal the packet.

3. Repeat to make 3 more foil packets. Place the packets in a slow cooker in a single layer, or stack them if needed.

4. Cover the cooker and cook for 4 to 6 hours on Low heat.

5. Be careful when serving: Very hot steam will release when you open the foil packets. Drizzle each opened packet with lemon juice for serving.

INGREDIENT TIP: Get creative with the vegetables in this recipe; other suggestions include bell peppers and green beans.

Per Serving: Calories: 210; Total fat: 5g; Sodium: 187mg; Carbohydrates: 17g; Fiber: 3g; Sugar: 9g; Protein: 30g

HERBED TUNA STEAKS

SERVES 4 // PREP TIME: 10 MINUTES // COOK TIME: 4 TO 6 HOURS ON LOW

Tuna is a great source of protein. Not only that, it is also low in calories and contains almost no fat, which makes it a good weight-loss option. Serve these tuna steaks with a simple salad and a side of cooked brown rice for an easy, healthy meal.

Nonstick cooking spray

4 (1-inch-thick) fresh tuna steaks (about 2 pounds total)

1 teaspoon sea salt

¼ teaspoon freshly ground black pepper

2 teaspoons extra-virgin olive oil

2 teaspoons dried thyme

2 teaspoons dried rosemary

1. Coat a slow-cooker insert with cooking spray, or line the bottom and sides with parchment paper or aluminum foil.

2. Season the tuna steaks all over with salt and pepper and place them in the prepared slow cooker in a single layer. Drizzle with the olive oil and sprinkle with the thyme and rosemary.

3. Cover the cooker and cook for 4 to 6 hours on Low heat.

INGREDIENT TIP: This recipe is delicious when you use fresh herbs. Use 4 thyme sprigs and 4 rosemary sprigs in place of the dried herbs, and discard them before serving.

Per Serving: Calories: 339; Total fat: 5g; Sodium: 689mg; Carbohydrates: 1g; Fiber: 1g; Sugar: 0g; Protein: 68g

SHRIMP AND FISH CHOWDER

SERVES 4 // PREP TIME: 20 MINUTES // COOK TIME: 4 TO 6 HOURS ON LOW, PLUS 15 TO 30 MINUTES ON LOW FOR THE SEAFOOD

This is an easy recipe that uses readily available ingredients. Make this a fish chowder using all fish instead of half fish and half shrimp. Or make it all shrimp—this recipe can be tailored to suit your preferences. You can use either fresh or frozen shrimp, but if they are frozen, they should be thawed first.

3 cups low-sodium vegetable broth

1 (28-ounce) can no-salt-added crushed tomatoes

1 large bell pepper, any color, seeded and diced

1 large onion, diced

2 zucchini, chopped

3 garlic cloves, minced

1 teaspoon dried thyme

1 teaspoon dried basil

½ teaspoon sea salt

¼ teaspoon freshly ground black pepper

¼ teaspoon red pepper flakes

8 ounces whole raw medium shrimp, peeled and deveined

8 ounces fresh cod fillets, cut into 1-inch pieces

1. In a slow cooker, combine the vegetable broth, tomatoes, bell pepper, onion, zucchini, garlic, thyme, basil, salt, black pepper, and red pepper flakes. Stir to mix well.

2. Cover the cooker and cook for 4 to 6 hours on Low heat.

3. Stir in the shrimp and cod. Replace the cover on the cooker and cook for 15 to 30 minutes on Low heat, or until the shrimp have turned pink and the cod is firm and flaky.

VARIATION TIP: Make this a heartier meal by stirring in 1 cup cooked brown rice once the cook time is complete.

Per Serving: Calories: 201; Total fat: 1g; Sodium: 598mg; Carbohydrates: 24g; Fiber: 7g; Sugar: 13g; Protein: 26g

RED SNAPPER WITH PEPPERS AND POTATOES

SERVES 4 // PREP TIME: 15 MINUTES // COOK TIME: 4 TO 6 HOURS ON LOW

Red snapper is a good source of protein that is low in calories but rich in essential vitamins. Here it pairs wonderfully with potatoes and herbs.

1 pound red potatoes, chopped

1 green bell pepper, seeded and sliced

1 red bell pepper, seeded and sliced

½ onion, sliced

1 (15-ounce) can no-salt-added diced tomatoes

⅓ cup whole Kalamata olives, pitted

5 garlic cloves, minced

1 teaspoon dried thyme

1 teaspoon dried rosemary

Juice of 1 lemon

Sea salt

Freshly ground black pepper

1½ to 2 pounds fresh red snapper fillets

2 lemons, thinly sliced

¼ cup chopped fresh parsley

1. In a slow cooker, combine the potatoes, green and red bell peppers, onion, tomatoes, olives, garlic, thyme, rosemary, and lemon juice. Season with salt and black pepper. Stir to mix well.

2. Nestle the snapper into the vegetable mixture in a single layer, cutting it into pieces to fit if needed. Top it with lemon slices.

3. Cover the cooker and cook for 4 to 6 hours on Low heat, or until the potatoes are tender.

4. Garnish with fresh parsley for serving.

INGREDIENT TIP: Good substitutes for snapper include trout, grouper, or sea bass.

Per Serving: Calories: 350; Total fat: 5g; Sodium: 241mg; Carbohydrates: 41g; Fiber: 8g; Sugar: 8g; Protein: 45g

LEMON-DILL SALMON

Salmon in the slow cooker produces perfectly cooked results with minimal effort. With just a few ingredients, this recipe is not only easy but also healthy. Serve this foolproof salmon at your next holiday meal or add it to your Sunday dinner rotation.

Nonstick cooking spray

2 pounds fresh salmon fillets

2 teaspoons extra-virgin olive oil

Sea salt

Freshly ground black pepper

2 garlic cloves, minced

¼ cup fresh dill, loosely chopped

1 lemon, thinly sliced

1. Generously coat a slow-cooker insert with cooking spray, or line the bottom and sides with parchment paper or aluminum foil.
2. Rub the salmon all over with olive oil and season it with salt, pepper, garlic, and dill. Place the salmon in the prepared slow cooker in a single layer, cutting it into pieces to fit if needed. Top it with lemon slices.
3. Cover the cooker and cook for 2 to 4 hours on Low heat.

INGREDIENT TIP: Use dried dill or another herb you prefer instead of fresh dill. An Italian seasoning blend can also be substituted.

Per Serving: Calories: 481; Total fat: 26g; Sodium: 108mg; Carbohydrates: 3g; Fiber: 1g; Sugar: 0g; Protein: 56g

ITALIAN BACCALÀ

SERVES 4 // PREP TIME: 2 TO 3 HOURS (10 MINUTES ACTIVE PREP)
COOK TIME: 4 TO 6 HOURS ON LOW

Baccalà is Italian for dried salt cod. Italian baccalà is a traditional recipe usually served around the Christmas holiday. The fish is rinsed, soaked in water, and drained, so it is mild and delicate in flavor and not overly salty, despite the name. This classic salt cod recipe can be served as a side dish or a main dish.

1½ pounds salt cod

1 (15-ounce) can no-salt-added diced tomatoes

½ onion, chopped

2 garlic cloves, minced

½ teaspoon red pepper flakes

¼ cup chopped fresh parsley, plus more for garnish

Juice of ½ lemon

1. Wash the salt cod to remove any visible salt. Completely submerge the cod in a large bowl of water and let it soak for at least 2 to 3 hours. If you are soaking it for longer than 24 hours, change the water after 12 hours.

2. In a slow cooker, combine the tomatoes, onion, garlic, red pepper flakes, parsley, and lemon juice. Stir to mix well. Drain the cod and add it to the slow cooker, breaking it apart as necessary to make it fit.

3. Cover the cooker and cook for 4 to 6 hours on Low heat.

4. Garnish with the remaining fresh parsley for serving.

INGREDIENT TIP: If salt cod is unavailable, you can use regular fresh cod instead (frozen is not recommended for best results, but if that is all that is available, thaw it first). If you do use fresh cod, add it directly to the slow cooker without soaking it first.

Per Serving: Calories: 211; Total fat: 2g; Sodium: 179mg; Carbohydrates: 8g; Fiber: 2g; Sugar: 4g; Protein: 39g

Chicken with Olives and
Capers, page 105

POULTRY

CHICKEN SHAWARMA WRAPS

SERVES 4 // PREP TIME: 15 MINUTES // COOK TIME: 4 TO 6 HOURS ON LOW

Chicken shawarma is traditionally roasted on a slowly turning vertical rotisserie or spit, but this slow-cooker version is easier and still has all the flavor. Shawarma is usually served as a sandwich in pita bread.

1 small onion, sliced

2 pounds boneless, skinless chicken thighs, cut into 1½-inch-thick strips

3 tablespoons white vinegar

3 tablespoons freshly squeezed lemon juice

2 tablespoons extra-virgin olive oil

1 tablespoon water

3 garlic cloves, minced

2 teaspoons ground allspice

1 teaspoon sea salt

1 teaspoon ground nutmeg

1 teaspoon ground cardamom

1 teaspoon garlic powder

½ teaspoon freshly ground black pepper

½ teaspoon za'atar (optional)

¼ teaspoon ground cinnamon

¼ cup fresh parsley, minced

4 large pita breads

1. Put the onion in a slow cooker and top it with the chicken.
2. In a small bowl, whisk together the vinegar, lemon juice, olive oil, water, garlic, allspice, salt, nutmeg, cardamom, garlic powder, pepper, za'atar (if using), and cinnamon until blended. Pour the sauce into the slow cooker. Stir to mix well.
3. Cover the cooker and cook for 4 to 6 hours on Low heat.
4. Sprinkle the parsley over the chicken and serve the chicken in the pitas.

SERVING TIP: If you like, garnish this shawarma with diced tomato, red onion, cucumber, and tahini or tzatziki sauce.

Per Serving: Calories: 509; Total fat: 22g; Sodium: 1,230mg; Carbohydrates: 39g; Fiber: 3g; Sugar: 2g; Protein: 38g

CHICKEN WITH LEMON AND ARTICHOKES

SERVES 4 // PREP TIME: 10 MINUTES // COOK TIME: 6 TO 8 HOURS ON LOW

Artichokes are enjoyed in many Mediterranean countries. They have a mild flavor (often compared to asparagus) and pair well with citrus. In this recipe, chicken and artichokes cook in a light homemade lemon sauce.

2 pounds bone-in, skin-on chicken thighs

1 large onion, sliced

1 (15-ounce) can artichoke hearts, drained, rinsed, and chopped

¼ cup freshly squeezed lemon juice

1 tablespoon extra-virgin olive oil

3 garlic cloves, minced

2 teaspoons dried thyme

1 teaspoon sea salt

½ teaspoon freshly ground black pepper

1 lemon, thinly sliced

1. In a slow cooker, combine the chicken and onion. Top with the artichoke hearts.
2. In a small bowl, whisk together the lemon juice, olive oil, garlic, thyme, salt, and pepper. Pour the sauce into the slow cooker. Top the chicken with lemon slices.
3. Cover the cooker and cook for 6 to 8 hours on Low heat.

SERVING TIP: Serve this recipe with your preferred cooked rice—whether it is brown rice or "rice" made from cauliflower.

Per Serving: Calories: 558; Total fat: 38g; Sodium: 927mg; Carbohydrates: 13g; Fiber: 4g; Sugar: 3g; Protein: 41g

GREEK CHICKEN CASSEROLE

SERVES 6 // PREP TIME: 15 MINUTES // COOK TIME: 6 TO 8 HOURS ON LOW

Casseroles are one-pot recipes, and they seem to be popular in pretty much every country. This Greek casserole is easy to make, but you would not guess it from the delectable result. Colorful and flavorful, this vegetable-packed dish can be served at your next dinner party or even for a weeknight dinner.

3 pounds boneless, skinless chicken thighs

1 small onion, chopped

4 Roma tomatoes, chopped

1 (12-ounce) jar artichoke hearts, drained

1 cup sliced pitted Kalamata olives

1 tablespoon dried oregano

1 teaspoon sea salt

½ teaspoon freshly ground black pepper

½ cup low-sodium chicken broth

1 tablespoon extra-virgin olive oil

1 lemon, thinly sliced

¾ cup crumbled feta cheese

2 tablespoons chopped fresh parsley

1. Place the chicken in the bottom of a slow cooker.
2. Add the onion, tomatoes, artichoke hearts, olives, oregano, salt, and pepper.
3. In a small bowl, whisk together the chicken broth and olive oil to combine. Pour the liquid over the chicken and vegetables and top with the lemon slices.
4. Cover the cooker and cook for 6 to 8 hours on Low heat.
5. Garnish with feta and fresh parsley for serving.

INGREDIENT TIP: If you want to use boneless, skinless chicken breasts, reduce the cook time by 1 to 2 hours since white meat cooks faster than dark meat.

Per Serving: Calories: 405; Total fat: 24g; Sodium: 1,201mg; Carbohydrates: 13g; Fiber: 3g; Sugar: 6g; Protein: 37g

TUSCAN TURKEY

SERVES 4 // PREP TIME: 15 MINUTES // COOK TIME: 6 TO 8 HOURS ON LOW

Food from Italy's Tuscany region is revered as some of the best in the country. I used turkey for a unique spin on this common dish, which is usually made with chicken. This Tuscan Turkey is a cheesy, herbed dish that is easy to make and a recipe that the entire family will enjoy. I like to serve this over cooked pasta or rice.

1 pound new potatoes, halved

1 red bell pepper, seeded and sliced

1 small onion, sliced

4 boneless, skinless turkey breast fillets (about 2 pounds)

1 cup low-sodium chicken broth

½ cup grated Parmesan cheese

3 garlic cloves, minced

1 teaspoon dried oregano

1 teaspoon dried rosemary

½ teaspoon sea salt

½ teaspoon freshly ground black pepper

½ teaspoon dried thyme

¼ cup chopped fresh basil

1. In a slow cooker, combine the potatoes, bell pepper, and onion. Stir to mix well.
2. Place the turkey on top of the vegetables.
3. In a small bowl, whisk together the chicken broth, Parmesan cheese, garlic, oregano, rosemary, salt, black pepper, and thyme until blended. Pour the sauce over the turkey.
4. Cover the cooker and cook for 6 to 8 hours on Low heat.
5. Garnish with fresh basil for serving.

VARIATION TIP: Make this dish creamier by stirring in 1 cup of plain Greek yogurt. Or, in a small bowl, stir 1 tablespoon flour or cornstarch in 2 tablespoons of water until the starch dissolves, add the mixture to the slow cooker, and cook for 5 to 10 minutes on Low heat, or until the sauce has thickened to your liking.

Per Serving: Calories: 402; Total fat: 5g; Sodium: 673mg; Carbohydrates: 24g; Fiber: 3g; Sugar: 3g; Protein: 65g

SHREDDED CHICKEN SOUVLAKI

SERVES 6 // PREP TIME: 10 MINUTES // COOK TIME: 6 TO 8 HOURS ON LOW

Souvlaki consists of skewered marinated meat, usually lamb. It is a simple dish that is common in Greece, where it can be found served everywhere—from fast-food places to fine-dining restaurants. This recipe uses chicken, which is cooked until tender and shredded rather than served on a skewer.

3 pounds boneless, skinless chicken thighs

⅓ cup water

⅓ cup freshly squeezed lemon juice

¼ cup red wine vinegar

4 garlic cloves, minced

2 tablespoons extra-virgin olive oil

2 teaspoons dried oregano

¼ teaspoon sea salt

¼ teaspoon freshly ground black pepper

1. In a slow cooker, combine the chicken, water, lemon juice, vinegar, garlic, olive oil, oregano, salt, and pepper. Stir to mix well.
2. Cover the cooker and cook for 6 to 8 hours on Low heat.
3. Transfer the chicken from the slow cooker to a work surface. Using 2 forks, shred the chicken, return it to the slow cooker, mix it with the sauce, and keep it warm until ready to serve.

INGREDIENT TIP: You can substitute boneless, skinless chicken breasts here if you prefer. If you do, reduce the cook time by 1 hour or so because white meat cooks faster than dark meat.

Per Serving: Calories: 462; Total fat: 28g; Sodium: 626mg; Carbohydrates: 3g; Fiber: 1g; Sugar: 1g; Protein: 48g

CHICKEN CAPRESE CASSEROLE

SERVES 4 // PREP TIME: 10 MINUTES // COOK TIME: 6 TO 8 HOURS ON LOW,
PLUS 10 TO 20 MINUTES ON LOW FOR THE CHEESE

Caprese is a simple Italian salad made of tomatoes, mozzarella, and basil. This chicken caprese recipe has all the usual caprese ingredients, but it is slow-cooked in casserole form. Use chicken thighs rather than breast meat because they will not dry out during the long cook time.

2 pounds boneless, skinless chicken thighs, cut into 1-inch cubes

1 (15-ounce) can no-salt-added diced tomatoes

2 cups fresh basil leaves (about 1 large bunch)

¼ cup extra-virgin olive oil

2½ tablespoons balsamic vinegar

½ teaspoon sea salt

⅛ teaspoon freshly ground black pepper

2 cups shredded mozzarella cheese

1. In a slow cooker, layer the chicken, tomatoes, and basil.
2. In a small bowl, whisk together the olive oil, vinegar, salt, and pepper until blended. Pour the dressing into the slow cooker. Stir to mix well.
3. Cover the cooker and cook for 6 to 8 hours on Low heat.
4. Sprinkle the mozzarella cheese on top. Replace the cover on the cooker and cook for 10 to 20 minutes on Low heat, or until the cheese melts.

SERVING TIP: Enjoy this chicken caprese casserole as is or serve it over cooked pasta or rice.

Per Serving: Calories: 569; Total fat: 40g; Sodium: 958mg; Carbohydrates: 9g; Fiber: 2g; Sugar: 4g; Protein: 47g

MEDITERRANEAN ROASTED TURKEY BREAST

SERVES 4 // PREP TIME: 15 MINUTES // COOK TIME: 6 TO 8 HOURS ON LOW

Jazz up your next Thanksgiving with this Mediterranean-inspired turkey. Lean protein is a staple in the Mediterranean diet. The recipe calls for a 4- to 6-pound turkey breast because anything larger will be hard to fit into a 6-quart slow cooker.

3 garlic cloves, minced

1 teaspoon sea salt

1 teaspoon dried oregano

½ teaspoon freshly ground black pepper

½ teaspoon dried basil

½ teaspoon dried parsley

½ teaspoon dried rosemary

½ teaspoon dried thyme

¼ teaspoon dried dill

¼ teaspoon ground nutmeg

2 tablespoons extra-virgin olive oil

2 tablespoons freshly squeezed lemon juice

1 (4- to 6-pound) boneless or bone-in turkey breast

1 onion, chopped

½ cup low-sodium chicken broth

4 ounces whole Kalamata olives, pitted

1 cup sun-dried tomatoes (packaged, not packed in oil), chopped

1. In a small bowl, stir together the garlic, salt, oregano, pepper, basil, parsley, rosemary, thyme, dill, and nutmeg.

2. Drizzle the olive oil and lemon juice all over the turkey breast and generously season it with the garlic-spice mix.

3. In a slow cooker, combine the onion and chicken broth. Place the seasoned turkey breast on top of the onion. Top the turkey with the olives and sun-dried tomatoes.

4. Cover the cooker and cook for 6 to 8 hours on Low heat.

5. Slice or shred the turkey for serving.

INGREDIENT TIP: Do not worry if you are missing any of the seasonings listed—just leave them out.

Per Serving: Calories: 761; Total fat: 55g; Sodium: 3,547mg; Carbohydrates: 20g; Fiber: 3g; Sugar: 10g; Protein: 83g

TURKEY PICCATA

Piccata is an Italian dish traditionally made with veal. In the United States, it is more commonly made with chicken. Substituting turkey is a fun way to switch up the recipe—and of course, use chicken if you like. A 6-quart slow cooker is best for this recipe.

1½ pounds new potatoes, halved

2 pounds boneless, skinless turkey breast fillets or thighs

1 cup low-sodium chicken broth

Juice of 2 lemons

1 tablespoon extra-virgin olive oil

¼ cup drained capers

1 teaspoon sea salt

1 teaspoon dried parsley

¼ teaspoon freshly ground black pepper

1 tablespoon unsalted butter, melted

2 tablespoons chopped fresh parsley

1. Put the potatoes in a slow cooker and place the turkey on top of the potatoes.

2. In a small bowl, whisk together the chicken broth, lemon juice, olive oil, capers, salt, parsley, pepper, and melted butter until combined. Pour this sauce over the turkey.

3. Cover the cooker and cook for 5 to 7 hours on Low heat.

4. Garnish with fresh parsley for serving.

PREPARATION TIP: To make this more of a traditional piccata, heat 1 tablespoon of extra-virgin olive oil in a large skillet over medium-high heat. Add the turkey and pan-sear it for 3 to 5 minutes per side until it has browned before adding to the slow cooker.

Per Serving: Calories: 427; Total fat: 8g; Sodium: 996mg; Carbohydrates: 30g; Fiber: 3g; Sugar: 4g; Protein: 60g

PESTO CHICKEN AND POTATOES

SERVES 6 // PREP TIME: 15 MINUTES // COOK TIME: 6 TO 8 HOURS ON LOW

Pesto is an Italian sauce made from fresh basil, pine nuts, salt, pepper, olive oil, and Parmesan cheese. You can tailor pesto sauce to your liking, which is why so many variations exist. This recipe uses an easy, homemade pesto sauce that slowly cooks on top of the chicken for a flavorful result.

FOR THE PESTO

1 cup fresh basil leaves

1 garlic clove, crushed

¼ cup pine nuts

¼ cup grated Parmesan cheese

2 tablespoons extra-virgin olive oil, plus more as needed

1 teaspoon sea salt

½ teaspoon freshly ground black pepper

FOR THE CHICKEN

Nonstick cooking spray

2 pounds red potatoes, quartered

3 pounds boneless, skinless chicken thighs

½ cup low-sodium chicken broth

TO MAKE THE PESTO

In a food processor, combine the basil, garlic, pine nuts, Parmesan cheese, olive oil, salt, and pepper. Pulse until smooth, adding more olive oil ½ teaspoon at a time if needed until any clumps are gone. Set aside.

TO MAKE THE CHICKEN

1. Coat a slow-cooker insert with cooking spray and put the potatoes into the prepared slow cooker.
2. Place the chicken on top of the potatoes.
3. In a medium bowl, whisk together the pesto and broth until combined and pour the mixture over the chicken.
4. Cover the cooker and cook for 6 to 8 hours on Low heat.

INGREDIENT TIP: Don't have time to make your own pesto? Use a store-bought version! Pesto should be readily available at your local grocery store.

Per Serving: Calories: 467; Total fat: 24g; Sodium: 819mg; Carbohydrates: 25g; Fiber: 3g; Sugar: 3g; Protein: 38g

TURKEY KOFTA CASSEROLE

SERVES 4 // PREP TIME: 20 MINUTES // COOK TIME: 6 TO 8 HOURS ON LOW

Kofta, kufta, kafta . . . it is spelled differently in different countries and languages. Regardless, the basic concept is the same—balls of ground meat mixed with spices and onion. The combination is very simple but packed with flavor. This basic casserole uses only kofta patties, potatoes, and tomato sauce—that's it. And do not think it is going to be bland, because it is not—the kofta's seasoning really gives this dish a punch.

FOR THE KOFTA

2 pounds raw ground turkey

1 small onion, diced

3 garlic cloves, minced

2 tablespoons chopped fresh parsley

1 tablespoon ground coriander

2 teaspoons ground cumin

1 teaspoon sea salt

1 teaspoon freshly ground black pepper

½ teaspoon ground nutmeg

½ teaspoon dried mint

½ teaspoon paprika

FOR THE CASSEROLE

Nonstick cooking spray

4 large (about 2½ pounds) potatoes, peeled and cut into ¼-inch-thick rounds

4 large (about 3 pounds) tomatoes, cut into ¼-inch-thick rounds

Salt

Freshly ground black pepper

1 (8-ounce) can no-salt-added, no-sugar-added tomato sauce

TO MAKE THE KOFTA

1. In a large bowl, mix together the turkey, onion, garlic, parsley, coriander, cumin, salt, pepper, nutmeg, mint, and paprika until combined.

2. Form the kofta mixture into 13 to 15 equal patties, using about 2 to 3 tablespoons of the meat mixture per patty.

TO MAKE THE CASSEROLE

1. Coat a slow-cooker insert with cooking spray.

2. Layer the kofta patties, potatoes, and tomatoes in the prepared slow cooker, alternating the ingredients as you go, like a ratatouille. Season with salt and pepper.

3. Spread the tomato sauce over the ingredients.

4. Cover the cooker and cook for 6 to 8 hours on Low heat, or until the potatoes are tender.

INGREDIENT TIP: Substitute your preferred ground meat for the ground turkey. Lean beef, chicken, or pork can all be used for flavorful results.

Per Serving: Calories: 588; Total fat: 17g; Sodium: 833mg; Carbohydrates: 61g; Fiber: 11g; Sugar: 6g; Protein: 52g

LEMON GARLIC CHICKEN

SERVES 6 // PREP TIME: 10 MINUTES // COOK TIME: 6 TO 8 HOURS ON LOW

Sometimes simple is best. The sauce for this lemon garlic chicken uses only lemon, garlic, broth, olive oil, salt, and pepper, plus an herb of your choice. Serve this recipe year-round for any occasion and know that you are not only keeping things simple and delicious, but healthy, too.

3 pounds boneless, skinless chicken thighs

½ cup low-sodium chicken broth

¼ cup freshly squeezed lemon juice

4 garlic cloves, minced

1 teaspoon grated lemon zest

1 teaspoon extra-virgin olive oil

1 teaspoon sea salt

½ teaspoon freshly ground black pepper

½ teaspoon dried thyme, parsley, or basil (or other herb of your choice)

1. In a slow cooker, combine the chicken, chicken broth, lemon juice, garlic, lemon zest, olive oil, salt, pepper, and your preferred herb. Stir to mix well.

2. Cover the cooker and cook for 6 to 8 hours on Low heat.

VARIATION TIP: Make the sauce creamy by stirring 1 tablespoon of flour or starch into 2 tablespoons of water in a small bowl until the starch dissolves; stir this thickener into the slow cooker and cook for 5 to 10 minutes on Low heat, or until the sauce has thickened to your liking.

Per Serving: Calories: 187; Total fat: 10g; Sodium: 607mg; Carbohydrates: 2g; Fiber: <1g; Sugar: <1g; Protein: 22g

CHICKEN WITH OLIVES AND CAPERS

SERVES 4 // PREP TIME: 10 MINUTES // COOK TIME: 6 TO 8 HOURS ON LOW

Olives, capers, and a quick sauce made from red wine vinegar are the real stars of this chicken recipe. When this is done cooking, I like to remove the chicken from the cooker, put it under the broiler to crisp the skin, and top it with the sauce from the slow cooker.

2 pounds bone-in, skin-on chicken thighs or legs

1 (5¾-ounce) jar green olives, with juice

1 (3½-ounce) jar capers, with juice

2 tablespoons red wine vinegar

1 garlic clove, minced

1 teaspoon dried oregano

¼ teaspoon sea salt

⅛ teaspoon freshly ground black pepper

2 tablespoons chopped fresh basil

1. Put the chicken in a slow cooker and top it with the olives and their juice and the capers and their juice.
2. Pour the vinegar over the chicken and sprinkle the garlic, oregano, salt, and pepper on top.
3. Cover the cooker and cook for 6 to 8 hours on Low heat.
4. Garnish with fresh basil for serving.

INGREDIENT TIP: If you do not like dark meat, substitute chicken breast and reduce the cooking time by 1 hour or so since the white meat cooks faster than dark meat.

Per Serving: Calories: 553; Total fat: 40g; Sodium: 1,073mg; Carbohydrates: 1g; Fiber: 1g; Sugar: <1g; Protein: 39g

ROSEMARY CHICKEN AND POTATOES

SERVES 4 // PREP TIME: 10 MINUTES // COOK TIME: 6 TO 8 HOURS ON LOW

This is another simple chicken recipe that packs a flavorful punch. Rosemary is a fragrant herb native to the Mediterranean, and it is one of my favorite herbs to cook with. There are only a few ingredients in this recipe, including lots of rosemary.

2 pounds red potatoes, quartered

2½ pounds bone-in, skin-on chicken thighs

¼ cup low-sodium chicken broth

2 tablespoons dried rosemary

1 teaspoon sea salt

½ teaspoon freshly ground black pepper

2 tablespoons extra-virgin olive oil

1. Put the potatoes in a slow cooker and arrange the chicken on top. Pour the chicken broth over the chicken and potatoes.
2. Sprinkle the rosemary, salt, and pepper on top of the chicken and potatoes, and drizzle the chicken with the olive oil.
3. Cover the cooker and cook for 6 to 8 hours on Low heat.

INGREDIENT TIP: Use a few fresh rosemary sprigs instead of the dried rosemary; remove and discard them before serving.

Per Serving: Calories: 833; Total fat: 51g; Sodium: 843mg; Carbohydrates: 37g; Fiber: 5g; Sugar: 4g; Protein: 53g

DECONSTRUCTED GREEK CHICKEN KEBABS

SERVES 4 // PREP TIME: 20 MINUTES // COOK TIME: 6 TO 8 HOURS ON LOW

Chicken kebabs are a popular street food that can also be found in many restaurants around Greece. This casserole uses the same flavors, but of course, it is not served on a stick. I like to serve this chicken in a warm pita topped with tzatziki sauce (see tip).

2 pounds boneless, skinless chicken thighs, cut into 1-inch cubes

2 zucchini (nearly 1 pound), cut into 1-inch pieces

1 green bell pepper, seeded and cut into 1-inch pieces

1 red bell pepper, seeded and cut into 1-inch pieces

1 large red onion, chopped

2 tablespoons extra-virgin olive oil

2 tablespoons freshly squeezed lemon juice

1 tablespoon red wine vinegar

2 garlic cloves, minced

1 teaspoon sea salt

1 teaspoon dried oregano

½ teaspoon dried basil

½ teaspoon dried thyme

¼ teaspoon freshly ground black pepper

1. In a slow cooker, combine the chicken, zucchini, green and red bell peppers, onion, olive oil, lemon juice, vinegar, garlic, salt, oregano, basil, thyme, and black pepper. Stir to mix well.

2. Cover the cooker and cook for 6 to 8 hours on Low heat.

SERVING TIP: Serve with this easy homemade tzatziki sauce: In a medium bowl, whisk together 1 cup plain Greek yogurt; 1 English cucumber, seeded, finely grated, and drained; 2 garlic cloves, minced; the juice of 1 lemon; and 2 tablespoons chopped fresh dill until blended. Taste and season with salt and pepper and whisk again to combine.

Per Serving: Calories: 375; Total fat: 21g; Sodium: 909mg; Carbohydrates: 13g; Fiber: 4g; Sugar: 5g; Protein: 34g

CHICKEN WITH DATES AND ALMONDS

SERVES 4 // PREP TIME: 15 MINUTES // COOK TIME: 6 TO 8 HOURS ON LOW

This Moroccan-inspired chicken dish will fill your kitchen with wonderful aromas. It might not look like enough liquid is present when this starts cooking, but trust me, this recipe produces a delicious sauce you can pour over the chicken when it is done.

1 onion, sliced

1 (15-ounce) can reduced-sodium chickpeas, drained and rinsed

2½ pounds bone-in, skin-on chicken thighs

½ cup low-sodium chicken broth

2 garlic cloves, minced

1 teaspoon sea salt

1 teaspoon ground cumin

½ teaspoon ground ginger

½ teaspoon ground coriander

¼ teaspoon ground cinnamon

¼ teaspoon freshly ground black pepper

½ cup dried dates

¼ cup sliced almonds

1. In a slow cooker, gently toss together the onion and chickpeas.
2. Place the chicken on top of the chickpea mixture and pour the chicken broth over the chicken.
3. In a small bowl, stir together the garlic, salt, cumin, ginger, coriander, cinnamon, and pepper. Sprinkle the spice mix over everything.
4. Top with the dates and almonds.
5. Cover the cooker and cook for 6 to 8 hours on Low heat.

INGREDIENT TIP: The dates provide a lovely sweetness. If you prefer this dish less sweet, use dried apricots instead.

Per Serving: Calories: 841; Total fat: 48g; Sodium: 812mg; Carbohydrates: 41g; Fiber: 9g; Sugar: 19g; Protein: 57g

Braised Lamb Shanks,
page 117

LAMB, BEEF, AND PORK

HERBED LAMB MEATBALLS

SERVES 4 // PREP TIME: 10 MINUTES // COOK TIME: 6 TO 8 HOURS ON LOW

This easy meatball recipe is kid-friendly and makes a great weeknight dinner. Dried herbs give the meatballs tons of flavor without overpowering the lamb. You do not need to sear the meatballs beforehand—they can go into the tomato sauce raw. Serve this dish over cooked pasta, rice, or polenta, or with potatoes.

1 (28-ounce) can no-salt-added diced tomatoes

2 garlic cloves, minced, divided

1 pound raw ground lamb

1 small onion, finely diced, or 1 tablespoon dried onion flakes

1 large egg

2 tablespoons bread crumbs

1 teaspoon dried basil

1 teaspoon dried oregano

1 teaspoon dried rosemary

1 teaspoon dried thyme

1 teaspoon sea salt

½ teaspoon freshly ground black pepper

1. In a slow cooker, combine the tomatoes and 1 clove of garlic. Stir to mix well.

2. In a large bowl, mix together the ground lamb, onion, egg, bread crumbs, basil, oregano, rosemary, thyme, salt, pepper, and the remaining 1 garlic clove until all of the ingredients are well-blended. Shape the meat mixture into 10 to 12 (2½-inch) meatballs. Put the meatballs in the slow cooker.

3. Cover the cooker and cook for 6 to 8 hours on Low heat.

INGREDIENT TIP: If you prefer, use ground beef or turkey instead of lamb.

Per Serving: Calories: 406; Total fat: 28g; Sodium: 815mg; Carbohydrates: 16g; Fiber: 5g; Sugar: 8g; Protein: 23g

MOROCCAN LAMB ROAST

SERVES 6 // PREP TIME: 15 MINUTES // COOK TIME: 6 TO 8 HOURS ON LOW

Lamb, spices, and a few vegetables are all you need for this simple, healthy slow-cooker meal. Together, these ingredients bring the flavors of Morocco to your kitchen.

¼ cup low-sodium beef broth or low-sodium chicken broth

1 teaspoon dried ginger

1 teaspoon dried cumin

1 teaspoon ground turmeric

1 teaspoon paprika

1 teaspoon garlic powder

1 teaspoon red pepper flakes

½ teaspoon ground cinnamon

½ teaspoon ground coriander

½ teaspoon ground nutmeg

½ teaspoon ground cloves

½ teaspoon sea salt

½ teaspoon freshly ground black pepper

1 (3-pound) lamb roast

4 ounces carrots, chopped

¼ cup sliced onion

¼ cup chopped fresh mint

1. Pour the broth into a slow cooker.
2. In a small bowl, stir together the ginger, cumin, turmeric, paprika, garlic powder, red pepper flakes, cinnamon, coriander, nutmeg, cloves, salt, and black pepper. Rub the spice mix firmly all over the lamb roast. Put the lamb in the slow cooker and add the carrots and onion.
3. Top everything with the mint.
4. Cover the cooker and cook for 6 to 8 hours on Low heat.

INGREDIENT TIP: Don't like lamb? Use a beef roast instead. Chuck roast, rump roast, or round roast all work well with this recipe.

Per Serving: Calories: 601; Total fat: 39g; Sodium: 398mg; Carbohydrates: 4g; Fiber: 1g; Sugar: 1g; Protein: 56g

GREEK LAMB CHOPS

Lamb chops are made by cutting at an angle perpendicular to the spine, generating a single serving of meat that is traditionally cooked and served on the bone. Accompanied by a homemade Greek sauce, these lamb chops are a crowd-pleaser.

3 pounds lamb chops

½ cup low-sodium beef broth

Juice of 1 lemon

1 tablespoon extra-virgin olive oil

2 garlic cloves, minced

1 teaspoon dried oregano

1 teaspoon sea salt

½ teaspoon freshly ground black pepper

1. Put the lamb chops in a slow cooker.
2. In a small bowl, whisk together the beef broth, lemon juice, olive oil, garlic, oregano, salt, and pepper until blended. Pour the sauce over the lamb chops.
3. Cover the cooker and cook for 6 to 8 hours on Low heat.

INGREDIENT TIP: You can substitute a 3-pound bone-in or boneless lamb roast in place of the chops.

Per Serving: Calories: 325; Total fat: 13g; Sodium: 551mg; Carbohydrates: 1g; Fiber: <1g; Sugar: <1g; Protein: 47g

LAMB CHILI WITH LENTILS

SERVES 4 // PREP TIME: 10 MINUTES // COOK TIME: 6 TO 8 HOURS ON LOW

Chili is a recipe made for the low-and-slow cooking of the slow cooker. With Mediterranean ingredients such as lamb and lentils, this unique spin on chili is great comfort food. Like most chilis, this one is even better the next day!

1 tablespoon extra-virgin olive oil

2 pounds raw ground lamb

1 (28-ounce) can no-salt-added crushed tomatoes

2½ cups water

1 onion, finely chopped

1 green bell pepper, seeded and diced

¾ cup dried lentils, any color

2 garlic cloves, minced

1 tablespoon chili powder

1 tablespoon ground cumin

1½ teaspoons sea salt

1 teaspoon dried oregano

½ teaspoon freshly ground black pepper

1. Heat the olive oil in a large skillet over medium-high heat. Add the ground lamb and cook for 3 to 5 minutes, breaking up the meat with a spoon, until it has browned and is no longer pink. Drain any grease and transfer the lamb to a slow cooker.

2. Add the tomatoes, water, onion, bell pepper, lentils, garlic, chili powder, cumin, salt, oregano, and black pepper to the lamb. Stir to mix well.

3. Cover the cooker and cook for 6 to 8 hours on Low heat, or until the lentils are tender.

SERVING TIP: Top this chili with your favorite Mediterranean garnishes, such as crumbled feta cheese and fresh herbs like chopped chives or parsley.

Per Serving: Calories: 540; Total fat: 32g; Sodium: 1,504mg; Carbohydrates: 36g; Fiber: 15g; Sugar: 11g; Protein: 31g

ROSEMARY LEG OF LAMB

Leg of lamb is one of the most popular slow-cooker recipes for a reason—it is easy and produces succulent meat that falls off the bone. This recipe is a must for your next holiday dinner.

2 cups low-sodium beef broth

2 rosemary sprigs (optional)

1 (3- to 4-pound) bone-in lamb leg

1 tablespoon extra-virgin olive oil

3 large garlic cloves, minced

1½ teaspoons dried rosemary

1 teaspoon sea salt

½ teaspoon freshly ground black pepper

1. In a slow cooker, combine the beef broth and rosemary sprigs (if using).
2. Rub the lamb all over with olive oil and season it with garlic, rosemary, salt, and pepper. Add the lamb to the slow cooker.
3. Cover the cooker and cook for 8 to 10 hours on Low heat, or until the lamb is tender.

SERVING TIP: You can make a nice gravy out of the drippings from the slow cooker: Once the lamb is cooked, strain the juices into a small saucepan and place it over medium-high heat. In a small bowl, whisk together ¼ cup of all-purpose flour and ½ cup of water until smooth to make a slurry. Whisk the slurry into the cooking juices. Bring the mixture to a boil. Cook, stirring constantly, for 1 to 2 minutes until thickened.

Per Serving: Calories: 353; Total fat: 16g; Sodium: 535mg; Carbohydrates: 1g; Fiber: <1g; Sugar: 0g; Protein: 48g

BRAISED LAMB SHANKS

SERVES 4 // PREP TIME: 10 MINUTES // COOK TIME: 8 TO 10 HOURS ON LOW

A lamb shank is a cut of lamb taken from the lower section of the leg; it can be from the front legs (foreshank) or the back legs (hind shank). Lamb shank is a tough cut, which makes it perfect for the slow cooker. It is also very flavorful when slow-cooked until tender. Serve the lamb shanks with plenty of their sauce on top of polenta, mashed potatoes, or cooked rice, and garnish with fresh rosemary if desired.

1 onion, diced

1 (28-ounce) no-salt-added, whole peeled tomatoes, with juice

2 large carrots, diced

3 garlic cloves, minced

1 cup low-sodium beef broth

1 teaspoon sea salt

1 teaspoon dried rosemary

1 teaspoon dried thyme

4 lamb shanks (about 3 pounds)

1. In a slow cooker, combine the onion, tomatoes and their juice, carrots, garlic, beef broth, salt, rosemary, and thyme. Stir to mix well.

2. Nestle the lamb shanks into the tomato mixture.

3. Cover the cooker and cook for 8 to 10 hours on Low heat.

PREPARATION TIP: If you have time, enhance the look and flavor of the lamb by broiling the shanks. When the lamb shanks are finished cooking, remove them from the slow cooker and place on a baking sheet. Place the baking sheet under the broiler for 3 to 5 minutes or until skin is crisp to your liking.

Per Serving: Calories: 527; Total fat: 18g; Sodium: 1,014mg; Carbohydrates: 16g; Fiber: 4g; Sugar: 8g; Protein: 73g

BEEF MEATBALLS IN GARLIC CREAM SAUCE

SERVES 4 // PREP TIME: 15 MINUTES // COOK TIME: 6 TO 8 HOURS ON LOW, PLUS 15 TO 30 MINUTES ON LOW FOR THE YOGURT

Herbed beef meatballs are slow-cooked in a garlicky cream sauce in this aromatic slow-cooker recipe. Serve these family-friendly meatballs over your favorite cooked pasta or rice, and be sure to add more sauce on top.

FOR THE SAUCE

1 cup low-sodium vegetable broth or low-sodium chicken broth

1 tablespoon extra-virgin olive oil

2 garlic cloves, minced

1 tablespoon dried onion flakes

1 teaspoon dried rosemary

2 tablespoons freshly squeezed lemon juice

Pinch sea salt

Pinch freshly ground black pepper

FOR THE MEATBALLS

1 pound raw ground beef

1 large egg

2 tablespoons bread crumbs

1 teaspoon ground cumin

1 teaspoon salt

½ teaspoon freshly ground black pepper

TO FINISH

2 cups plain Greek yogurt

2 tablespoons chopped fresh parsley

TO MAKE THE SAUCE

In a medium bowl, whisk together the vegetable broth, olive oil, garlic, onion flakes, rosemary, lemon juice, salt, and pepper until combined.

TO MAKE THE MEATBALLS

In a large bowl, mix together the ground beef, egg, bread crumbs, cumin, salt, and pepper until combined. Shape the meat mixture into 10 to 12 (2½-inch) meatballs.

1. Pour the sauce into the slow cooker.

2. Add the meatballs to the slow cooker.

3. Cover the cooker and cook for 6 to 8 hours on Low heat.

4. Stir in the yogurt. Replace the cover on the cooker and cook for 15 to 30 minutes on Low heat, or until the sauce has thickened.

5. Garnish with fresh parsley for serving.

INGREDIENT TIP: To make this a low-carb or keto recipe, substitute almond flour for the bread crumbs in the meatballs.

Per Serving: Calories: 345; Total fat: 20g; Sodium: 842mg; Carbohydrates: 13g; Fiber: 1g; Sugar: 8g; Protein: 29g

ITALIAN SHORT RIB STEW

SERVES 4 OR 5 // PREP TIME: 15 MINUTES // COOK TIME: 6 TO 8 HOURS ON LOW

Short ribs are a cut of beef taken from the chuck, brisket, or rib area of cattle. I prefer to use short ribs from the chuck area; they seem to be the easiest to find at the grocery store. This savory dish combines Italian flavors and short ribs for a healthy, hearty stew.

3 pounds boneless beef short ribs, cut into 1-inch pieces

1½ pounds red potatoes, quartered

4 carrots, cut into ½-inch cubes

4 ounces mushrooms, sliced

1 large onion, diced

1 (28-ounce) can no-salt-added diced tomatoes

1 cup low-sodium beef broth

2 garlic cloves, minced

1 tablespoon dried thyme

1½ teaspoons dried parsley

1½ teaspoons sea salt

½ teaspoon freshly ground black pepper

1. In a slow cooker, combine the short ribs, potatoes, carrots, mushrooms, onion, tomatoes, beef broth, garlic, thyme, parsley, salt, and pepper. Stir to mix well.

2. Cover the cooker and cook for 6 to 8 hours on Low heat.

PREPARATION TIP: For extra flavor: In a large skillet over medium-high heat, brown the short ribs in 2 teaspoons of olive oil for a few minutes per side, in batches as needed, before adding them to the slow cooker.

Per Serving: Calories: 818; Total fat: 37g; Sodium: 1,371mg; Carbohydrates: 49g; Fiber: 10g; Sugar: 15g; Protein: 74g

OSSO BUCO

SERVES 4 // PREP TIME: 10 MINUTES // COOK TIME: 8 TO 10 HOURS ON LOW

Osso buco is Italian for "bone with a hole." It refers to the marrow hole at the center of the crosscut shank. Traditionally made with veal, this version uses beef because it is less expensive, easier to find, and better suited for the low-and-slow method of slow cooking. You can use up to 3 pounds of meat without needing to alter the recipe.

1 (15-ounce) can no-salt-added diced tomatoes

1 cup low-sodium beef broth

2 carrots, diced

1 small onion, diced

1 celery stalk, diced

2 garlic cloves, minced

1 teaspoon sea salt

2 to 3 pounds bone-in beef shanks

2 tablespoons Italian seasoning

Handful fresh parsley

1. In a slow cooker, combine the tomatoes, beef broth, carrots, onion, celery, garlic, and salt. Stir to mix well.
2. Generously season the beef shanks with the Italian seasoning. Nestle the shanks into the vegetable mixture.
3. Cover the cooker and cook for 8 to 10 hours on Low heat.
4. Garnish with fresh parsley for serving.

PREPARATION TIP: For extra flavor: In a large skillet over medium heat, sear the seasoned beef shanks in 2 teaspoons of olive oil for a few minutes per side, in batches as needed, before adding them to the slow cooker.

Per Serving: Calories: 303; Total fat: 11g; Sodium: 961mg; Carbohydrates: 22g; Fiber: 6g; Sugar: 9g; Protein: 28g

MOUSSAKA

SERVES 4 TO 6 // PREP TIME: 35 MINUTES (10 MINUTES ACTIVE PREP)
COOK TIME: 6 TO 8 HOURS ON LOW

Moussaka is a Mediterranean dish that is enjoyed in many countries, such as Greece and Turkey. It is traditionally made with ground lamb, eggplant, and tomatoes, but different countries have different variations. This slow-cooker version resembles the traditional Greek moussaka. Although the eggplant is usually fried, here it is not because, in a slow cooker, this results in soggy breaded eggplant. Traditionally, moussaka is topped with a béchamel sauce, but this recipe uses whipped ricotta as a healthier option.

3 eggplants, peeled and cut lengthwise into ½-inch-thick slices

1 teaspoon sea salt, plus more for salting the eggplant

1 (15-ounce) can no-salt-added crushed tomatoes

1 pound raw ground beef

1 small onion, diced

2 garlic cloves, minced

1 teaspoon dried oregano

½ teaspoon freshly ground black pepper

½ teaspoon dried basil

¼ teaspoon ground cinnamon

¼ teaspoon ground nutmeg

1½ cups grated Parmesan cheese

1 cup whipped ricotta

1. Lay the eggplant slices on paper towels in a single layer and lightly sprinkle them with salt. Let them sit for 10 to 30 minutes to draw out excess moisture. Blot the eggplant slices with a paper towel to remove the excess liquid and salt.
2. Put the tomatoes in a slow cooker and top them with half of the eggplant slices.
3. Spread the ground beef over the top of the eggplant. Top with the onion and garlic.
4. Sprinkle the salt, oregano, pepper, basil, cinnamon, and nutmeg over everything.
5. Cover everything with ¾ cup of Parmesan cheese and top with the remaining eggplant slices.
6. Spread the ricotta over the top and sprinkle with the remaining ¾ cup of Parmesan cheese.
7. Cover the cooker and cook for 6 to 8 hours on Low heat.
8. Let cool to room temperature before slicing and serving.

INGREDIENT TIP: Substitute chopped or ground lamb in place of the ground beef in this recipe.

Per Serving: Calories: 561; Total fat: 28g; Sodium: 1,471mg; Carbohydrates: 32g; Fiber: 11g; Sugar: 17g; Protein: 49g

KOFTA WITH VEGETABLES IN TOMATO SAUCE

SERVES 4 // PREP TIME: 15 MINUTES // COOK TIME: 6 TO 8 HOURS ON LOW

Kofta is a kind of meatball served in many Mediterranean countries. It usually consists of minced ground meat, onion, and spices. This dish deconstructs kebabs, combining kofta patties with kebab vegetables and slowly cooking them both in a delectable tomato sauce.

1 pound raw ground beef

1 small white or yellow onion, finely diced

2 garlic cloves, minced

1 tablespoon dried parsley

2 teaspoons ground coriander

1 teaspoon ground cumin

½ teaspoon sea salt

½ teaspoon freshly ground black pepper

¼ teaspoon ground nutmeg

¼ teaspoon dried mint

¼ teaspoon paprika

1 (28-ounce) can no-salt-added diced tomatoes

2 or 3 zucchini, cut into 1½-inch-thick rounds

4 ounces mushrooms

1 large red onion, chopped

1 green bell pepper, seeded and chopped

1. In large bowl, mix together the ground beef, white or yellow onion, garlic, parsley, coriander, cumin, salt, pepper, nutmeg, mint, and paprika until well combined and all of the spices and onion are well blended into the meat. Form the meat mixture into 10 to 12 oval patties. Set aside.

2. In a slow cooker, combine the tomatoes, zucchini, mushrooms, red onion, and bell pepper. Stir to mix well.

3. Place the kofta patties on top of the tomato mixture.

4. Cover the cooker and cook for 6 to 8 hours on Low heat.

Per Serving: Calories: 263; Total fat: 9g; Sodium: 480mg; Carbohydrates: 23g; Fiber: 7g; Sugar: 12g; Protein: 27g

MEDITERRANEAN PORK WITH OLIVES

SERVES 4 // PREP TIME: 10 MINUTES // COOK TIME: 6 TO 8 HOURS ON LOW

Olives and a lemony broth cook with pork chops for a simple and satisfying meal. The recipe calls for pork chops, but you can also use pork tenderloin or even a pork butt or shoulder. If you choose to substitute butt or shoulder, just shred the meat once it is cooked.

1 small onion, sliced

4 thick-cut, bone-in pork chops

1 cup low-sodium chicken broth

Juice of 1 lemon

2 garlic cloves, minced

1 teaspoon sea salt

1 teaspoon dried oregano

1 teaspoon dried parsley

½ teaspoon freshly ground black pepper

2 cups whole green olives, pitted

1 pint cherry tomatoes

1. Put the onion in a slow cooker and arrange the pork chops on top.

2. In a small bowl, whisk together the chicken broth, lemon juice, garlic, salt, oregano, parsley, and pepper. Pour the sauce over the pork chops. Top with the olives and tomatoes.

3. Cover the cooker and cook for 6 to 8 hours on Low heat.

INGREDIENT TIP: Use your favorite Mediterranean herbs instead of the oregano and parsley. Fresh herbs also work well with this recipe (use 3 tablespoons).

Per Serving: Calories: 293; Total fat: 18g; Sodium: 1,697mg; Carbohydrates: 6g; Fiber: 1g; Sugar: 3g; Protein: 22g

BALSAMIC PORK TENDERLOIN

SERVES 6 // PREP TIME: 10 MINUTES // COOK TIME: 6 TO 8 HOURS ON LOW

Pork tenderloin is a long thin cut, one of the most tender. Balsamic vinegar is a great complement to pork tenderloin, and this recipe uses an easy-to-make, balsamic-based sauce to slow-cook the meat. Slice or shred this succulent pork for serving.

1 small onion, sliced

1 (3-pound) pork tenderloin

1 cup balsamic vinegar

½ cup low-sodium beef broth

3 garlic cloves, crushed

2 tablespoons capers, undrained

1½ teaspoons olive oil

1 teaspoon dried rosemary

1 teaspoon sea salt

½ teaspoon freshly ground black pepper

1. Put the onion in a slow cooker and arrange the pork tenderloin on top.

2. In a small bowl, whisk together the vinegar, beef broth, garlic, capers, olive oil, rosemary, salt, and pepper until combined. Pour the sauce over the pork.

3. Cover the cooker and cook for 6 to 8 hours on Low heat.

Per Serving: Calories: 281; Total fat: 10g; Sodium: 523mg; Carbohydrates: 7g; Fiber: <1g; Sugar: <1g; Protein: 45g

BACON-WRAPPED STUFFED PORK

SERVES 4 // PREP TIME: 20 MINUTES // COOK TIME: 5 TO 7 HOURS ON LOW

The bacon provides most of the flavor, so not much other seasoning is needed. Use thick-cut bacon because it will hold up better during the long cooking time. For crispier bacon, remove the bacon-wrapped pork from the slow cooker once it has finished cooking and broil it for 2 to 3 minutes until the bacon turns crispy.

¼ cup sun-dried tomatoes (packaged, not packed in oil)

4 ounces feta cheese

2 garlic cloves, minced

1 teaspoon dried parsley

½ teaspoon sea salt

¼ teaspoon freshly ground black pepper

4 large boneless pork chops (about 2 pounds)

12 thick-cut bacon slices

Nonstick cooking spray

1. In a small bowl, stir together the sun-dried tomatoes, feta cheese, garlic, parsley, salt, and pepper until well-blended.
2. Cut each pork chop in half horizontally, leaving it attached at one side. Divide the filling among the chops, spreading it evenly on the inside of each.
3. Close the chops and wrap each one all the way around with 2 or 3 bacon slices, starting and finishing on the bottom of each chop.
4. Coat a slow-cooker insert with cooking spray.
5. Place the wrapped pork chops in the slow cooker in a single layer, snuggling them in as evenly as possible.
6. Cover the cooker and cook for 5 to 7 hours on Low heat.

INGREDIENT TIP: Substitute chicken breasts for the pork chops if desired and follow the recipe as written.

Per Serving: Calories: 477; Total fat: 29g; Sodium: 2,239mg; Carbohydrates: 4g; Fiber: 1g; Sugar: 3g; Protein: 45g

PORK CASSEROLE WITH FENNEL AND POTATOES

SERVES 6 // PREP TIME: 20 MINUTES // COOK TIME: 6 TO 8 HOURS ON LOW

Fennel is native to the Mediterranean region. Fennel bulbs can be roasted on their own, but here I pair them with potatoes and pork tenderloin for a more complete meal. Serve this casserole with a fresh vegetable, such as asparagus or broccoli, on the side.

2 large fennel bulbs

3 pounds pork tenderloin, cut into 1½-inch pieces

2 pounds red potatoes, quartered

1 cup low-sodium chicken broth

4 garlic cloves, minced

1½ teaspoons dried thyme

1 teaspoon dried parsley

1 teaspoon sea salt

Freshly ground black pepper

⅓ cup shredded Parmesan cheese

1. Cut the stalks off the fennel bulbs. Trim a little piece from the bottom of the bulbs to make them stable, then cut straight down through the bulbs to halve them. Cut the halves into quarters. Peel off and discard any wilted outer layers. Cut the fennel pieces crosswise into slices.

2. In a slow cooker, combine the fennel, pork, and potatoes. Stir to mix well.

3. In a small bowl, whisk together the chicken broth, garlic, thyme, parsley, and salt until combined. Season with pepper and whisk again. Pour the sauce over the pork.

4. Cover the cooker and cook for 6 to 8 hours on Low heat.

5. Top with Parmesan cheese for serving.

VARIATION TIP: To make a creamy sauce: When the cook time is complete, stir in ½ cup of plain Greek yogurt. Replace the cover on the cooker and cook for 5 to 10 minutes on Low heat, or until the sauce has thickened.

Per Serving: Calories: 918; Total fat: 30g; Sodium: 1,001mg; Carbohydrates: 46g; Fiber: 8g; Sugar: 4g; Protein: 109g

Lemon Olive Oil Cake,
page 134

DESSERTS

DECONSTRUCTED BAKLAVA

SERVES 6 // PREP TIME: 10 MINUTES // COOK TIME: 3 TO 5 HOURS ON LOW

When people think of Greek desserts, baklava is usually the first one that comes to mind. While traditional baklava cannot be made in the slow cooker, this dessert has all the flavors of baklava that you love.

1 pound phyllo dough, thawed enough to slice but still a little frozen

1 pound chopped nuts of your choice

½ cup honey

⅓ cup sugar

1 teaspoon vanilla extract

1 teaspoon ground cinnamon

1 cup (2 sticks) unsalted butter, melted

1. Line the bottom and sides of a slow-cooker insert with parchment paper or aluminum foil.
2. Unroll the phyllo dough and cut it into 2-inch pieces. Transfer the pieces to a large bowl and add the nuts, honey, sugar, vanilla, and cinnamon. Stir to mix well. Pour the mixture into the prepared slow cooker.
3. Pour the melted butter on top.
4. Cover the cooker and cook for 3 to 5 hours on Low heat.

INGREDIENT TIP: Use your favorite nuts for this recipe; I prefer chopped walnuts.

Per Serving: Calories: 1,121; Total fat: 85g; Sodium: 585mg; Carbohydrates: 85g; Fiber: 7g; Sugar: 37g; Protein: 17g

CUMIN POACHED PEARS

Poached pears come together quickly for an easy, elegant dessert. Use a firm pear like Bosc, D'Anjou, or Concorde because they are more likely to hold their shape during slow cooking. The addition of cumin makes these pears more savory than sweet; add more honey to sweeten this dish if you prefer. Serve these pears chilled or warm, and save the sauce to pour over the top of the cooked pears.

6 pears, peeled, cored, and quartered

1 cup water

¼ cup honey

1½ teaspoons ground cinnamon

1 teaspoon ground cumin

½ teaspoon ground cloves

1. Put the pears in a slow cooker.
2. In a small bowl, whisk together the water, honey, cinnamon, cumin, and cloves until combined. Pour the sauce over the pears.
3. Cover the cooker and cook for 3 to 5 hours on Low heat, or until the pears are tender.

SERVING TIP: Serve these pears with your favorite toppings like raisins or dried cranberries. This is great served with frozen sliced bananas.

Per Serving: Calories: 190; Total fat: 1g; Sodium: 3mg; Carbohydrates: 50g; Fiber: 7g; Sugar: 42g; Protein: 1g

LEMON OLIVE OIL CAKE

SERVES 6 // PREP TIME: 15 MINUTES // COOK TIME: 3 TO 5 HOURS ON LOW

Light and lemony, this is a Mediterranean version of a classic French cake. Extra-virgin olive oil and yogurt combine to create this moist, delicate dessert. Top this cake with the optional lemon glaze or eat it as is.

FOR THE CAKE

Nonstick cooking spray

1½ cups all-purpose flour

1½ cups whole-wheat flour

1 tablespoon baking powder

1 teaspoon salt

1¼ cups coconut palm sugar

4 large eggs

Grated zest of 1 lemon

Juice of 1 lemon

1¼ cups mild-flavored, extra-virgin olive oil

1 cup plain whole-milk yogurt

FOR THE LEMON GLAZE (OPTIONAL)

2 cups sugar

2 tablespoons freshly squeezed lemon juice

1 tablespoon plain Greek yogurt

TO MAKE THE CAKE

1. Generously coat a slow-cooker insert with cooking spray.

2. In a large bowl, combine the all-purpose and whole-wheat flours, baking powder, and salt, and stir thoroughly.

3. In another large bowl, whisk together the sugar, eggs, lemon zest, and lemon juice until the sugar is fully dissolved and the mixture is frothy (reserve a pinch of the lemon zest for the glaze, if using). Whisk in the olive oil and yogurt until well-combined.

4. Stir the flour mixture into the wet ingredients until combined and no dry flour remains. Pour the batter into the prepared slow cooker.

5. Cover the cooker and cook for 3 to 5 hours on Low heat, or until the center of the cake is done and a knife inserted into it comes out clean.

6. Let the cake cool before drizzling the glaze on top (if using).

TO MAKE THE LEMON GLAZE (IF USING)

In a large bowl, whisk together the sugar, lemon juice, and yogurt until smooth. Drizzle over the cooled cake. Garnish with lemon zest if desired.

INGREDIENT TIP: Use a milder-flavored olive oil so that its taste does not overpower the cake.

Per Serving: Calories: 726; Total fat: 50g; Sodium: 714mg; Carbohydrates: 61g; Fiber: 5g; Sugar: 15g; Protein: 13g

What Is Coconut Palm Sugar?

Coconut palm sugar, also known simply as coconut sugar, is an alternative to refined white sugar. Coconut palm sugar is made by heating the sap of the coconut flower until most of the water has evaporated. The result is an unprocessed, granulated sugar with a color that is similar to brown sugar. Coconut sugar can be bought in several different forms, including granulated crystals, a syrup, or a soft paste. For the recipes in this cookbook, you will need the granulated crystal form.

Is Coconut Palm Sugar Healthier?

Overall, coconut palm sugar and granulated white sugar have a similar nutritional profile. Unlike refined sugar, coconut palm sugar contains significant minerals like calcium, magnesium, and iron. Pure coconut palm sugar also has a lower glycemic index than refined sugar, meaning that it does not cause your blood sugar levels to spike and drop rapidly after consumption. While coconut palm sugar is not a weight-loss tool, it is a healthier option, particularly for diabetics.

Using Coconut Palm Sugar in Baking

Coconut palm sugar can be substituted with refined white sugar using a 1:1 ratio. That means you can use either one without any adjustments to the recipe. When you bake with coconut palm sugar, keep in mind that it tastes similar to brown sugar or molasses, and it will sometimes turn your batter brown as well. Depending on the recipe and your tastes, you might want to use refined white sugar instead.

Where Can You Buy Coconut Palm Sugar?

These days, coconut palm sugar is available at most grocery stores, particularly high-end ones. It can also be found at health-food stores or online.

ZUCCHINI BREAD

SERVES 4 TO 6 // PREP TIME: 15 MINUTES // COOK TIME: 3 TO 5 HOURS ON LOW

Zucchini is popular in Mediterranean cooking and in many recipes in this book. If you find yourself with some leftover zucchini hanging around, this is the perfect recipe to use it up. Zucchini bread is easy to make, and it can be enjoyed at any time of day.

Nonstick cooking spray

3 large eggs

2 cups coconut palm sugar

1 cup extra-virgin olive oil

2½ teaspoons vanilla extract

2½ cups grated zucchini (from about 2 zucchini)

2½ cups whole-wheat flour

2½ teaspoons ground cinnamon

2 teaspoons baking powder

1 teaspoon baking soda

1. Generously coat a slow-cooker insert with cooking spray, or line the bottom and sides with parchment paper or aluminum foil.
2. In a medium bowl, whisk together the eggs, sugar, olive oil, and vanilla until well-blended.
3. Add the zucchini, flour, cinnamon, baking powder, and baking soda. Stir to mix well. Pour the batter into the prepared slow cooker.
4. Cover the cooker and cook for 3 to 5 hours on Low heat, or until the middle has set and a knife inserted into it comes out clean.

INGREDIENT TIP: If you do not have whole-wheat flour on hand, substitute all-purpose flour in the same amount and follow the recipe as written.

Per Serving: Calories: 933; Total fat: 59g; Sodium: 662mg; Carbohydrates: 93g; Fiber: 11g; Sugar: 34g; Protein: 16g

ITALIAN APPLE CAKE

SERVES 4 TO 6 // PREP TIME: 15 MINUTES // COOK TIME: 3 TO 5 HOURS ON LOW

In Italy, this dessert is known as *torta di mele*. It is a popular Italian dessert made with fresh apples cooked in a simple cake batter. Use your preferred apple; I like to use a sweet apple, like Red Delicious or Gala.

Nonstick cooking spray

3 large eggs

1 cup coconut palm sugar

1 cup milk of your choice

4 tablespoons unsalted butter, at room temperature

1¼ cups all-purpose flour

1¼ cups whole-wheat flour

1 tablespoon baking powder

4 large apples, finely diced

1. Generously coat a slow-cooker insert with cooking spray, or line the bottom and sides with parchment paper or aluminum foil.

2. In a large bowl, using a handheld electric mixer, beat the eggs, sugar, milk, and butter until smooth.

3. Stir in the all-purpose and whole-wheat flours, baking powder, and apples until well-mixed. Pour the batter into the prepared slow cooker.

4. Cover the cooker and cook for 3 to 5 hours on Low heat, or until the center is completely done and a knife inserted into it comes out clean.

VARIATION TIP: Add 2 ounces of your favorite chopped nut to the batter before pouring it into the slow cooker.

Per Serving: Calories: 611; Total fat: 16g; Sodium: 553mg; Carbohydrates: 106g; Fiber: 11g; Sugar: 42g; Protein: 17g

MEDITERRANEAN RICE PUDDING

SERVES 4 TO 6 // PREP TIME: 10 MINUTES // COOK TIME: 3 TO 5 HOURS ON LOW

Rice pudding has been around a long time and variations exist all over the world. In this Mediterranean version, I use ground cardamom, a very aromatic spice that is a little minty, a little citrusy, and a little spicy. If you do not like spicy, cut the amount of cardamom in half and add some cinnamon in its place.

½ cup long-grain brown rice, rinsed

4 cups milk of your choice

¼ cup coconut palm sugar

3 tablespoons unsalted butter, melted

1 tablespoon ground cardamom

1 teaspoon vanilla extract

1. In a slow cooker, combine the rice, milk, sugar, butter, cardamom, and vanilla. Stir until the sugar is dissolved.
2. Cover the cooker and cook for 3 to 5 hours on Low heat, or until the rice is tender.

SERVING TIP: Top this rice pudding with chopped nuts or fresh fruit.

Per Serving: Calories: 279; Total fat: 12g; Sodium: 187mg; Carbohydrates: 34g; Fiber: 1g; Sugar: 15g; Protein: 10g

CHOCOLATE OLIVE OIL CAKE

SERVES 4 TO 6 // PREP TIME: 10 MINUTES // COOK TIME: 3 TO 5 HOURS ON LOW

This basic chocolate cake is full of surprises. In addition to the chocolate, the real key to this recipe is a mild-tasting olive oil, which makes the cake moist without overpowering the chocolate flavor.

Nonstick cooking spray

1½ cups coconut palm sugar

½ cup all-purpose flour

½ cup whole-wheat flour

½ cup cocoa powder

¼ teaspoon baking soda

¼ teaspoon salt

1 cup water

⅔ cup mild-flavored, extra-virgin olive oil

3 large eggs

1 teaspoon vanilla extract

1. Generously coat a slow cooker with cooking spray, or line the bottom and sides with parchment paper or aluminum foil.

2. In a large bowl, whisk together the sugar, all-purpose and whole-wheat flours, cocoa powder, baking soda, and salt.

3. Add the water, olive oil, eggs, and vanilla, and whisk together until well-combined. Pour the batter into the prepared slow cooker.

4. Cover the cooker and cook for 3 to 5 hours on Low heat, or until the middle has set and a knife inserted into it comes out clean.

SERVING TIP: Top this cake with powdered sugar and serve with a dollop of vanilla Greek yogurt.

Per Serving: Calories: 587; Total fat: 41g; Sodium: 310mg; Carbohydrates: 52g; Fiber: 6g; Sugar: 25g; Protein: 10g

SLOW-COOKED FRUIT MEDLEY

SERVES 4 TO 6 // PREP TIME: 10 MINUTES // COOK TIME: 3 TO 5 HOURS ON LOW

This is another great technique-based, adaptable recipe, like the Steamed Vegetables on page 65. And it helps you effortlessly eat more delicious fruit! I purposely left the ingredients vague because you can use any fruit you like in this recipe—strawberries, peaches, figs, whatever you have—or even a combination. Just put the fruit in the slow cooker with a couple of extra ingredients and you are done.
One of my favorite combinations is a berry medley of strawberries, raspberries, and blueberries.

Nonstick cooking spray

1 pound fresh or frozen fruit of your choice, stemmed and chopped as needed

⅓ cup almond milk or low-sugar fruit juice of your choice

½ cup honey

1. Generously coat a slow cooker with cooking spray, or line the bottom and sides with parchment paper or aluminum foil.
2. In a slow cooker, combine the fruit and milk. Gently stir to mix.
3. Drizzle the fruit with the honey.
4. Cover the cooker and cook for 3 to 5 hours on Low heat.

VARIATION TIP: Sprinkle 8 ounces of chopped nuts over the top of this medley before cooking for a nutty-crust topping.

Per Serving: Calories: 192; Total fat: <1g; Sodium: 27mg; Carbohydrates: 50g; Fiber: 3g; Sugar: 45g; Protein: 1g

FIG AND ALMOND YELLOW CAKE

If figs are in season, this is the recipe to make. Although it is listed in the dessert section, this cake can also be served for brunch. I like to drizzle some honey on top of each slice before serving.

Nonstick cooking spray

½ cup plus 2 tablespoons all-purpose flour

½ cup plus 2 tablespoons whole-wheat flour

¼ cup coconut palm sugar

1 teaspoon baking powder

¼ teaspoon ground cinnamon

3 large eggs

4 tablespoons butter, at room temperature

1 teaspoon almond extract

8 fresh figs, stemmed and halved

1. Generously coat a slow cooker with cooking spray, or line the bottom and sides with parchment paper or aluminum foil.

2. In a large bowl, whisk together the all-purpose and whole-wheat flours, sugar, baking powder, and cinnamon.

3. In another large bowl, whisk together the eggs, butter, and almond extract until well-combined.

4. Add the dry ingredients to the wet ingredients and mix until well-blended. Pour the batter into the prepared slow cooker.

5. Arrange the fig halves on top of the batter.

6. Cover the cooker and cook for 3 to 5 hours on Low heat, or until the middle has set and a knife inserted into it comes out clean.

INGREDIENT TIP: Substitute 4 ounces dried figs, dried apricots, dates, or even prunes for the fresh figs in this recipe.

Per Serving: Calories: 377; Total fat: 16g; Sodium: 263mg; Carbohydrates: 53g; Fiber: 6g; Sugar: 20g; Protein: 10g

MEDITERRANEAN ORANGE YOGURT CAKE

SERVES 4 TO 6 // PREP TIME: 10 MINUTES // COOK TIME: 3 TO 5 HOURS ON LOW

Yogurt cake is traditionally a part of French cuisine, but here it has a Mediterranean spin. In addition to the olive oil, Greek yogurt is added to the batter and that results in an extra-moist cake. Fresh orange juice and zest provide a subtle citrus touch. Serve this warm or at room temperature.

Nonstick cooking spray

¾ cup all-purpose flour

¾ cup whole-wheat flour

2 teaspoons baking powder

¼ teaspoon salt

1 cup coconut palm sugar

½ cup plain Greek yogurt

½ cup mild-flavored, extra-virgin olive oil

3 large eggs

2 teaspoons vanilla extract

Grated zest of 1 orange

Juice of 1 orange

1. Generously coat a slow cooker with cooking spray, or line the bottom and sides with parchment paper or aluminum foil.
2. In a large bowl, whisk together the all-purpose and whole-wheat flours, baking powder, and salt.
3. In another large bowl, whisk together the sugar, yogurt, olive oil, eggs, vanilla, orange zest, and orange juice until smooth.
4. Add the dry ingredients to the wet ingredients and mix together until well-blended. Pour the batter into the prepared slow cooker.
5. Cover the cooker and cook for 3 to 5 hours on Low heat, or until the middle has set and a knife inserted into it comes out clean.

SERVING TIP: Once the cake has cooled, top it with powdered sugar or vanilla Greek yogurt.

Per Serving: Calories: 544; Total fat: 33g; Sodium: 482mg; Carbohydrates: 53g; Fiber: 4g; Sugar: 19g; Protein: 11g

The Dirty Dozen and the Clean Fifteen™

A nonprofit environmental watchdog organization called Environmental Working Group (EWG) looks at data supplied by the US Department of Agriculture (USDA) and the Food and Drug Administration (FDA) about pesticide residues. Each year it compiles a list of the best and worst pesticide loads found in commercial crops. You can use these lists to decide which fruits and vegetables to buy organic to minimize your exposure to pesticides and which produce is considered safe enough to buy conventionally. This does not mean they are pesticide-free, though, so wash these fruits and vegetables thoroughly. The list is updated annually, and you can find it online at EWG.org/FoodNews.

DIRTY DOZEN™

1. strawberries
2. spinach
3. kale
4. nectarines
5. apples
6. grapes
7. peaches
8. cherries
9. pears
10. tomatoes
11. celery
12. potatoes

†Additionally, nearly three-quarters of hot pepper samples contained pesticide residues.

CLEAN FIFTEEN™

1. avocados
2. sweet corn*
3. pineapples
4. sweet peas (frozen)
5. onions
6. papayas*
7. eggplants
8. asparagus
9. kiwis
10. cabbages
11. cauliflower
12. cantaloupes
13. broccoli
14. mushrooms
15. honeydew melons

*A small amount of sweet corn, papaya, and summer squash sold in the United States is produced from genetically modified seeds. Buy organic varieties of these crops if you want to avoid genetically modified produce.

Measurement Conversions

VOLUME EQUIVALENTS (LIQUID)

US STANDARD	US STANDARD (OUNCES)	METRIC (APPROXIMATE)
2 tablespoons	1 fl. oz.	30 mL
¼ cup	2 fl. oz.	60 mL
½ cup	4 fl. oz.	120 mL
1 cup	8 fl. oz.	240 mL
1½ cups	12 fl. oz.	355 mL
2 cups or 1 pint	16 fl. oz.	475 mL
4 cups or 1 quart	32 fl. oz.	1 L
1 gallon	128 fl. oz.	4 L

VOLUME EQUIVALENTS (DRY)

US STANDARD	METRIC (APPROXIMATE)
$\frac{1}{8}$ teaspoon	0.5 mL
¼ teaspoon	1 mL
½ teaspoon	2 mL
¾ teaspoon	4 mL
1 teaspoon	5 mL
1 tablespoon	15 mL
¼ cup	59 mL
$\frac{1}{3}$ cup	79 mL
½ cup	118 mL
$\frac{2}{3}$ cup	156 mL
¾ cup	177 mL
1 cup	235 mL
2 cups or 1 pint	475 mL
3 cups	700 mL
4 cups or 1 quart	1 L

OVEN TEMPERATURES

FAHRENHEIT	CELSIUS (APPROXIMATE)
250°F	120°C
300°F	150°C
325°F	165°C
350°F	180°C
375°F	190°C
400°F	200°C
425°F	220°C
450°F	230°C

WEIGHT EQUIVALENTS

US STANDARD	METRIC (APPROXIMATE)
½ ounce	15 g
1 ounce	30 g
2 ounces	60 g
4 ounces	115 g
8 ounces	225 g
12 ounces	340 g
16 ounces or 1 pound	455 g

Resources

BOOKS

Make Every Day Mediterranean: An Oldways 4-Week Menu Plan, Oldways Preservation and Exchange Trust, 2017.
This is a straightforward introduction to Mediterranean menu planning that makes it easy to adapt to the Mediterranean lifestyle.

Mediterranean Diet Meal Prep: Easy and Healthy Mediterranean Diet Recipes to Prep, Grab, and Go, Brandon Hearn, 2019.
This is an easy-to-read resource with simple recipes made with ingredients that can be found in your local grocery store. It also includes numerous meal prep samples and guides to help you plan and adapt your eating style to the Mediterranean diet.

The Complete Mediterranean Cookbook: 500 Vibrant, Kitchen-Tested Recipes for Living and Eating Well Every Day, America's Test Kitchen, 2016.
This book contains more than 500 recipes focused solely on the Mediterranean diet. From appetizers and soups to desserts, it contains recipes for every dietary need and cooking style.

The *Mediterranean Diet for Beginners: The Complete Guide—40 Delicious Recipes, 7-Day Diet Meal Plan, and 10 Tips for Success*, Rockridge Press, 2013.
This is great for anyone beginning the Mediterranean diet; it provides thorough coverage of the basics of the diet with recipes and sample meal plans.

The Mediterranean Diet Weight Loss Solution: The 28-Day Kickstart Plan for Lasting Weight Loss, Julene Stassou, 2017.
Written by a registered dietician, this book specializes in how to use the Mediterranean diet for weight loss. It includes more than 90 recipes along with exercise and weight-loss tips.

WEBSITES

Healthline.com: www.healthline.com/nutrition/mediterranean-diet-meal-plan

This quick reference covers the Mediterranean diet for beginners and includes a basic overview of what you can and cannot eat along with a sample meal plan.

Mediterranean Living: www.mediterraneanliving.com/mediterranean-diet-resources

This website specializes in everything Mediterranean, with a large section on the Mediterranean diet that includes links to Mediterranean recipes, bloggers, authors, diet plans, and exercise programs.

The Mediterranean Dish: www.themediterraneandish.com/resources

This popular blog specializes in the Mediterranean diet and includes an extensive recipe archive; you can also find basic spices to fill your pantry and shopping lists.

U.S. News and World Report: health.usnews.com/best-diet/mediterranean-diet

This website specifically addresses the "hows" of the Mediterranean diet, including how to follow it, how to lose weight on it, how much it will cost, and other information, with links to additional references.

WebMD: www.webmd.com/diet/a-z/the-mediterranean-diet

This overview of the Mediterranean diet outlines why it is healthy and how to get started on it.

Recipe Index

Index

Acknowledgments

To my husband Lawrence—thank you for your unconditional support.
Once again, thank you to Callisto Media for this opportunity.
Specifically, I would like to thank Wes for bringing this cookbook to
my attention, and Laura Bryn and Mary for being great editors.
You all made this process as easy as it could be.

About the Author

SHANNON EPSTEIN is a full-time food and travel writer. This is her fourth cookbook. Shannon lives in Los Angeles with her husband and dog.

CPSIA information can be obtained
at www.ICGtesting.com
Printed in the USA
LVHW070416020120
642306LV00016B/399/P